FIREA.
CURIC

Charles Noé Daly, wearing cuirass with nineteen pistols. Photograph
courtesy Stephen V. Grancsay.

FIREARMS
CURIOSA

by Lewis Winant

ISHI PRESS INTERNATIONAL

Firearms Curiosa
by
Lewis Winant

First published in 1954

Published several times since

Current Edition Printed in December, 2009
Ishi Press in New York and Tokyo

Library of Congress Catalog Card Number 54-7114

ISBN 4-87187-871-6
978-4-87187-871-5

Ishi Press International
1664 Davidson Avenue, Suite 1B
Bronx NY 10453-7877
USA

1-917-507-7226

Printed in the United States of America

Firearms Curiosa by Lewis Winant

Foreword by Mario L. Sacripante

This book is filled with pictures of rare, strange and unusual guns, firearms and other weapons.

It has much sought after antique guns that were invented but are forgotten today, strange looking weapons like the **Reed Weapon**, invented by my friend Mr. **Reed**.

It has **knuckle-dusters**, guns with only a cylinder you can hit a man with after you have run out of bullets.

It has a photo of the gun that killed **U.S. President James A. Garfield** on **July 2, 1881**. The gun has no barrel so it can be held without being seen.

Lewis Winant was a major dealer and collector of firearms. He assembled here more than **300 pieces**.

The many strange and freakish gun fabrications that are shown in this book are a tribute to man's inventive energy as applied to the development of arms. From days just past and from days long gone, Lewis Winant has selected over 300 pieces as representative of the oddities that have been constructed to utilize the propelling force of gunpowder.

There are pistols in **knives and canes; pistols in flashlights, purses, plows, whips, bicycle handlebars, stirrups, keys, pipes, belts, sundials, and other contrivances**. In addition there are other types classified as **oddities**, such as **squeezers, knuckle-dusters, alarm and trap**. There are **combination weapons, turret, chain and harmonica pistols**, guns using superposed loads and other **variations from the norm**. These remarkable firearms come from more than fifty collections.

Foreword by Mario L. Sacripante

Some of the most interesting **rarities** have never before been illustrated in any publication, and their existence is unknown to most collectors.

Collectors of **Colt revolvers** and **Elgin pistols** will find items of special interest to them. *Firearm Curiosa* will delight the serious collector and will entertain the many who have little knowledge of firearms but who will be fascinated by the singular and sometimes fantastic products of man's creativeness. Those with an inventive turn of mind will treasure the book. Both professional and amateur inventors will find stimulation in the variations in employment and technical functions of the weapons.

Firearms Curiosa has been welcome to students and collectors, for previously there has existed not one single compendium of reliable information covering **odd firearms**.

Mario L. Sacripante
New York
December 1, 2009

CONTENTS

FOREWORD

Many people helped me with this book. To the several collectors who helped me very greatly and whose names appear many times as owners of guns illustrated let me say that none finished better than second, in my estimate of who gave me the most help.

First place goes to my wife, Florence Winant, who helped with the photography, with the searching, with constructive suggestions for phrasing of descriptions, and who did nearly all the typing.

All of the collectors, dealers, and others who are here listed, cooperated with me in supplying actual guns, photographs of guns, other material or data. The names of owners of the guns illustrated appear under the illustrations except in the case of guns owned by me when photographed. The reader will observe that the names of some men who have extensive collections are frequently repeated in the captions. Those men gave most important assistance. Other men supplied perhaps only one or two guns for illustration, but some of those guns were notable and unique, and all were contributions much appreciated.

My sincere thanks go to:

Robert Abels
John L. Barry, Jr.
Harold Berger
Frank E. Bivens, Jr.
Edmund Budde, Jr.
Murray M. Citrin
Joseph W. Desserich
F. Theodore Dexter
Anthony A. Fidd
Anthony Fidd, Jr.
Mrs. Albert Foster
Paul S. Foster
H. Gordon Frost
Dr. W. R. Funderburg
Herb Glass
Dr. James S. Golden, Jr.
Stephen V. Grancsay
G. Charter Harrison
Leonard A. Heinrich
Calvin Hetrick
John Hintlian
Thomas T. Hoopes
Frank R. Horner
Hampton P. Howell, Jr.
Major Leo E. Huff
George N. Hyatt
Stephen Ickes
C. Stanley Jacob
Osborne Klavestad
W. G. C. Kimball

Joseph Kindig, Jr.
Harry C. Knode
William M. Locke
Thomas J. McHugh
John C. McMurray
Arnott J. Millett
Paul Mitchell
W. Keith Neal
George R. Numrich, Jr.
John E. Parsons
Governor Gordon Persons
Oscar J. Rees
Eddie Reider
Glode M. Requa
Martin B. Retting
Raymond L. J. Riling
Frank Russell
James E. Serven
Major Hugh Smiley
Sam E. Smith
Henry M. Stewart
George Umphrey
John K. Watson
Leo J. Werner
Caleb J. Westergard
Paul J. Westergard
Frank Wheeler
J. S. White
Rev. W. E. Woosnam-Jones
Harold G. Young

7

I wish to acknowledge that I received friendly co-operation and valuable assistance from officers, representatives, and employees of various companies and institutions here and abroad. I wish to mention particularly—Colt's Manufacturing Company, of Hartford, Connecticut; the Library of Congress, the Smithsonian Institution, the National Archives, the United States Patent office, of Washington, D. C.; the Metropolitan Museum of Art, the New York Historical Society, the New York Public Library, of New York City; the Newark Public Library, the New Jersey Historical Society of Newark, New Jersey.

Curiosa is a term that embraces variations from custom not always spoken of as oddities. I settled for *Firearms Curiosa* as a title because there are disagreements as to what are or are not firearms oddities. It is often fully as impossible to analyze a gun to determine why or if it is an oddity, as to analyze a joke to determine why or if it is funny.

With a few controversial or misunderstood guns I have gone to considerable length, but in general I have confined descriptions of oddity guns to their radical features and have omitted minutiae such as barrel lengths, types of rifling if any, even calibers.

The photographs were taken at various times and places, by both amateur and professional photographers. Where a shoulder gun is shown on the same page with a pistol or revolver it is improbable the illustrations will be on the same scale. Where two or more short guns are shown on the same page they will be roughly to scale, with the length of one or another sometimes given. No sizes will be given in the case of pocket knives, pipes, and canes which are of ordinary dimensions.

Chapter 1

COMBINATION WEAPONS

OF ALL PECULIAR FIREARMS the most unbelievable have resulted from man's fondness for combining a gun with something else.

Firearms combined with edged weapons, such as knives, seem reasonable. Pistols combined with table forks seem ill-devised, but they exist. In fact, there is one instance—I believe one only—where a small flintlock pistol was built into a spoon as well as into the companion pieces, the knife and fork.°

Guns have been built into purses, canes, police truncheons, flash lights, cameras, and even sundials, with some reason. They have also been built into wrenches, pipes, helmets, stirrups and fish hooks. We shall come to those later.

In starting with combination weapons it may be well to point out that only weapons combined with guns are shown. There are many other forms of combined weapons, such as spears combined with axes, and swords with throwing knives in the scabbards. In this volume no piece is shown that is not capable of shooting, using powder as a propellant. Any miniature pistol, or any tinderlighter for that matter, that is illustrated, can shoot.

We usually think of a combination weapon as combining a gun with another weapon designed for offense. One of the very early combinations was of a pistol and a weapon of defense.

° Illustration #267

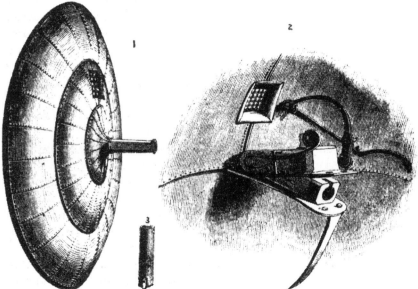

Obverse.   Fig. 55—Pistol Shield.   Reverse.

1. Matchlock buckler—diameter 18½″/ Metropolitan Museum of Art
   collection..

2. Drawing from Greener's *The Gun and Its Development*.

Illustration #1 shows a shield, or buckler, with a built-in matchlock pistol. Enough of these shields to outfit at least a company of men-at-arms were made in England early in the 16th century. The shield is made of wood faced with steel plates, and is about 18½″ in diameter. The pistol barrel is about 6″ long, having about half its length protruding from the front of the shield. Ignition is by means of a slow match, which is a slowly burning fuse made of chemically impregnated rope. The gun is breechloading, using vented cartridge-like steel casings loaded with powder and ball. These steel chambers have no obturating power, but otherwise they function just like the separate primed metallic cartridges used in the nineteenth century by the well known 1865 model Maynard rifles. Illustration #2 is a reproduction of a drawing in Greener's *The Gun and its Development* which shows the mechanism better than a photograph. On the left is the outer side of the shield and the muzzle of the gun. On the right is the inner side of the shield and the breech of the barrel ready to receive the cartridge which is shown separately in the illustration. To quote Greener—"The system adopted for loading consists of a block hinged upon each side of the barrel: it is raised up for the insertion of a loaded thimble or steel chamber. The match was affixed to a serpentine attached to a rod stapled to the interior of the shield, which was depressed by hand into the flash-pan upon the top (of the lowered block) to ignite the charge".

What looks like a barred window is no more than that—just a grating that may be opened or closed.

A soldier carrying a supply of the loaded cartridges should be able to fire a gun of this construction rapidly, once the match was alight and fastened to the serpentine. Very few motions are necessary to raise the block, withdraw a fired casing, insert a loaded casing, press down the hinged block, and then press down the serpentine. A modern single shot hammer-type shotgun without an automatic ejector might not be fired more rapidly.

Probably only one in twenty gun collectors has seen one of these "gonne shields". The one illustrated is in this country's top public museum collection of fine firearms. However, other similar shields are in private collections in this country and in Europe. Occasionally one goes on the auction block or finds its way into a dealer's hands. Probably the largest number of these shields to be found in a single collection is in the Tower of London. There were ten there in 1916 according to the Charles Ffoulkes inventory. Ffoulkes reports the inventory of 1547 showed forty.

Some of the pieces illustrated in this book are easily obtained by collectors who want unusual guns. Nearly all—of which photographic prints are shown—even a "gonne shield"—can be acquired by a patient collector. A few pieces are unique. It is very probable there is no other example of the combination weapon which is illustrated in Figure 3 and also in the frontispiece. This is another, but quite different, combination of shield and gun. The first was a buckler, held by the forearm, equipped with one matchlock pistol. This is a cuirass, fastened around the body, equipped with nineteen cartridge pistols. It was "found in Bordeaux, 1917", and was in the collection of the famed Charles Noé Daly from that time until it was sold at auction June 5, 1935 in Toronto. It weighed thirty pounds.

I quote a description supplied by Stephen V. Grancsay, Curator of Arms and Armor, The Metropolitan Museum of Art, New York City—"Cuirass of steel on which have been mounted nineteen similar pistols, which may be dropped for loading, and when brought into a right angle position may be fired in batteries of four and five by pressing the studs and levers, which release the hammers which are cocked by a hook carried on a chain. This remarkable effort to create a human arsenal is accompanied by a pair of stirrups, each of which contains two pistols, dischargeable by the pulling of a strap in the event of pursuit or attack. Undoubtedly the most remarkable freak in the line of small arms extant, and the life work of some French armourer of the first order."

The just described stirrups are companion pieces to the cuirass. They are shown in illustration 4 and also in the two illustrations where Mr. Daly is pictured wearing the cuirass, carrying the stirrups in the left hand and a large combination knife-revolver in the right.

Now we turn to firearms combined with other weapons designed for offense rather than defense. Simple attachments to firearms, such as bayonets to muskets, daggers to pistols, or

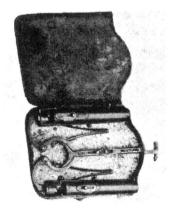

3. Another view of Charles Noé Daly/ Courtesy Stephen V. Grancsay.

4. Stirrup pistols/ Photograph courtesy Joseph Kindig, Jr.

nightsticks to revolvers, are not included, but still the list is long.

Early guns were mostly single shot, and reloading was a slow process. They could not be surely depended upon to go off when desired. They were unfair and unchivalrous in the eyes of the knights. The knights were dismayed by "the murderous intent comprised in villainous saltpetre",* but they could not ignore this hated invention. The men-at-arms soon accepted guns as auxiliaries to be built into cutting, thrusting, and clubbing weapons.

The very early hand firearm, simply a steel tube with a touch hole, was often primarily a mace. The mounted men-at-arms who could command the services of the best armourers were soon carrying at their saddle bows, instead of the usual maces, such elaborate weapons as those shown in illustrations 5 and 6. Both are Holy Water Sprinklers, made long ago in Germany. Figure 5 is the first form. It is a mace with four separate steel barrels, each 9" long. These barrels are formed into a wooden cylinder held with four iron bands, two of which have six spikes each. The ignition system is that used before any gun lock was invented, and consists of touching a slow burning "match", or other tinder, held by the hand, to the powder in the touch hole. There is a touch hole with a sliding cover for each barrel. The muzzle has a hinged spear-topped iron cap, held in place by a hook. When the touch holes and the muzzle are all covered this first of pepperboxes is completely concealed within the mace. In the illustration one vent cover is shown open.

Figure 6 shows one of these multishot combination weapons equipped with gun locks. There is a matchlock for each of the four barrels. The gun powder is still ignited by the glowing match cord, but now the match, instead of being held by the hand, is fixed in the end of a curved holder, the serpentine, and mechanically moved down to the touch hole by pressure on a button trigger on the side of the lock plate.

Students are not in full agreement as to the correct name for these mace combinations, though they have been known as Holy Water Sprinklers for four hundred years. One item in the inventory made in the year 1547 of the weapons in the Tower of

---

* Rudyard Kipling, ARITHMETIC ON THE FRONTIER.

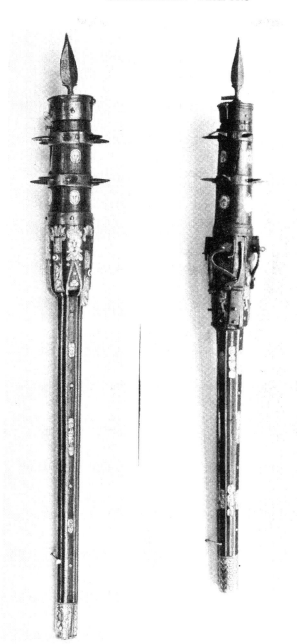

5. Holy Water Sprinkler—36" overall/ Joseph Kindig, Jr. collection.

6. Holy Water Sprinkler/ Metropolitan Museum of Art collection.

London was "Holly water sprincles wt thre gonnes in the Topp". Many students think the name derives from a fancied resemblance to an aspergillum, but Joseph Skelton, in *Meyrick's Ancient Armour,* states, "To sprinkle the holy water was the cantphrase for fetching blood, which will account for the appellation, as there is no resemblance between the weapon and the aspergillum."

The matchlock mace combinations were made of wood with fanciful bone inlays and iron fittings. They were followed by maces equipped with wheel lock pistols, often made entirely of iron or steel. Figure 7 illustrates an all-metal Saxon mace, circa 1550, decorated with etched and gilded designs. The handle of the mace encloses a foot long barrel which has its muzzle at the mace's spiked end. This piece possesses the great advantage that in sudden emergency it does not require having at hand a slow match already alight in order to shoot. The wheel lock can be kept for hours or days ready to shoot at pressure on the trigger.

It is assumed the reader is no stranger to either the conventional flintlock or the later percussion firearms. To those not familiar with the complicated but very efficient wheel locks it may be said they are similar to flintlocks in that they ignite powder by developing sparks by friction—but in the wheel lock, steel moves against flint, whereas in the much simpler flintlock, which includes the miquelet and the snaphaunce, flint moves against steel.

Illustration 8 is of a late 16th century dagger, probably German, combined with a wheel lock pistol. Except the wood grips the dagger is all metal completely covered with etching. There is a 2" tip which pulls out to disclose the pistol barrel.

Illustration 9 is of a German hunting sword with a bone-inlaid curved wooden stock, fitted with a late 17th century wheel lock. The knights thought the early guns unchivalrous. The later hunters sometimes condemned swords fitted with pistols as unsportsmanlike—that is when used against animals.

In figure 10 is shown a combination of a wheel lock pistol with a hunting knife, or "chopper." It is German of about 1540, decorated with foliation and gilding, with horn handles. A perpetual ecclesiastical calendar is etched on the blade. Any calen-

7. Wheel lock mace/ Metropolitan Museum of Art collection.

8. Wheel lock dagger/ Metropolitan Museum of Art collection.

9. Wheel lock sword/ Metropolitan Museum of Art collection.

dar sword is highly prized by a collector of valuable antiques. A calendar blade on a combination weapon is very rare.

In the first column of the table etched on the blade are the days of the month. In the next column are the days of the week, represented by the first seven letters of the alphabet, continuously repeated in sequence. In the third column the appropriate saint to whom to appeal is named for every day of the year.

A sword with a flint pistol is shown in figure 11. This is unusual in that the blade is the larger saber blade used by the military. The flintlock is the goose neck type, the most commonly used form of gun lock from about 150 up to 250 years ago. On this piece the barrel is just over 7" long, with a bore of .50 caliber. Most of the edged weapons which are in combination with flint pistols have shorter barrels and smaller caliber bores.

Swords, particularly hunting swords, fitted with single-shot flint pistols, were made in sufficiently large numbers to permit the present day collector to find one with little difficulty. Less easy to locate are swords with two pistols.

A fine Italian hunting sword made by Pietro Bruni, figure 12, has two .35 caliber flint pistols, one on each side of the blade. The illustration shows one pistol in cocked and the other in fired position. The triggers are small buttons in the hilt. In this piece, as in most hunting swords and knives, the pistol is aimed toward the point of the blade. In hunting boar the idea was to drive in the sword and then press the triggers.

That was not how the weapon in illustration 13 was designed to function. This has its pistol barrel pointing in the opposite direction. The knife thrust and the pistol shot would hardly occur simultaneously. The barrel is only 1½" long, and of only .25 caliber. Perhaps this piece, made around 1720, is a combination weapon designed primarily for personal defense, though having a hunting blade. The sheath is of leather, brass mounted. The handle, also of brass, is inscribed F. X. RICHTER IN NEJ. Of much interest is the lock. That has all its mechanism on the outside of the handle.

Another combination weapon with a very interesting lock is the highly ornamented Turkish over-and-under pistol, illustration 14, which has a slim double edged dagger concealed between its two slightly converging barrels. The hilt of the dagger is also

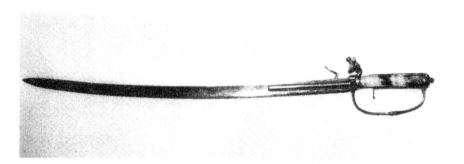

10. Calendar hunting knife/ Metropolitan Museum of Art collection.

11. Flintlock saber/ Harold G. Young collection.

12. Hunting sword/ Frank R. Horner collection.

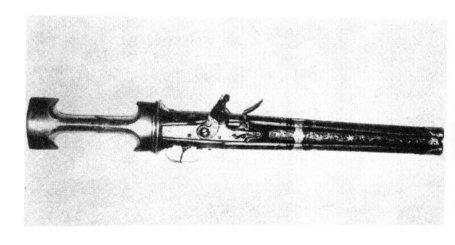

13. Hunting knife/ Major Leo E. Huff collection.

14. Dagger pistol—20" overall/ Eddie Reider collection.

the grip of the pistol. It is of silver, engraved, with the foot-long blade of steel, gold damascened. The wooden part of the stock is finely silver inlaid with floral designs. The barrels and the lock are gold decorated. The two barrels are fixed, not turn-over, and the lock appears to be designed for only a single shot pistol. However, drawing back the cock after the top barrel is fired, automatically pulls back an upper flash pan and discloses a second pan underneath with a vent leading to the lower barrel.

A crossbow and a wheel lock arquebus is a very rare combination. An excellent example is pictured in illustration 15. The crossbow is the hunting type called a prodd. It is of steel and shoots stones or pellets of lead.

It is to be noted that this weapon, which bears the Nuremberg mark and was made about the year 1600, has a set trigger for the wheel lock. The guard for this trigger looks like the conventional under the frame bow release. The actual bow release is mounted over the arquebus barrel, along with the nut designed to engage a bow string and the large steel lever for bending the bow, while a two-piece telescopic ramrod is in a channel under the barrel. The stock, of walnut, is richly incrusted with engraved bone representations of animals, masks and scrollwork. This is of course strictly a hunting weapon. The prodd is for very small game; the arquebus is for larger game.

In illustration 16 are shown two axes, 36" and 33" long respectively, a chopping knife 14" overall, and a sword 27" long—all combined with firearms.

Axes were popular weapons when firearms were first used. They were favorites for taking apart an unhorsed knight.

With the development of flintlocks the demand for combination weapons for combat was fast waning. Such pieces as the flintlock axe shown at the top of the illustration were made in small numbers. This particular piece has a stock of wood; axe, lock and barrel of steel; and furniture of brass. It comes apart at the wide brass band to permit withdrawal from the shaft of a short sword. The gun is fired by a button trigger which is equipped with a slide safety.

Next is a fine early wheel lock battle axe. This is a sturdy piece with a heavy blade and a rather large bore barrel. The stock is a completely inlaid work of art, with serpents and animal heads preponderant in the design.

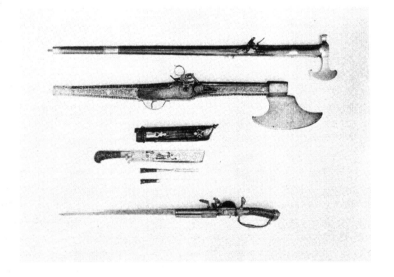

15. Wheel lock prodd/ Joseph Kindig, Jr. collection.

16. Group of weapons—14″ to 36″ overall/ Joseph Kindig, Jr. collection.

Between the wheel lock axe and the sword is shown a Saxon chopping knife, complete with the trousse and its accessories. This piece is outstanding. It is not only of superior workmanship, but in remarkably fine condition. The horn grips, the fine etching, and the original blue and gilding have come through four centuries in fine style. The illustration shows the small wheel lock. It does not show the part round, part octagon barrel which lies along the other side of the blade. The knife is designed for chopping meat after a stag hunt. The trousse, which sheaths the hunting knife, holds in addition to the small knife and fork shown, a combination rammer and spanner.

The sword with the single flintlock and the two pistol barrels is another unusual piece. As in the Turkish dagger combination (Illustration 14) the flash pan for the lower barrel is concealed under the pan for the top barrel. On this sword combination the sliding plate that must be pulled out to permit sparks to reach the vent in the lower barrel is not connected with the cock and must be drawn back manually. The pistol barrels, the lock plate, and the sword furniture are of brass. The decoration is very ornamental. The sword has a guard, an indication the weapon is intended for combat rather than hunting.

Illustration 17 shows the heads and parts of the hafts of four polearms. Each piece has a full length of approximately six feet.

Many gun features, such as rifled barrels, folding sights, set triggers, which we find on twentieth century guns, may also be found on sixteenth century guns. Such features alone are not criteria of a gun's age. Type of ignition is a guide in dating a gun, and guns are primarily classified by lock types. There are usually considered to be just four main types of locks made prior to the development of modern cartridge arms. These four main types are all shown here in this collection of polearms.

The early hand guns, around 1400, had no locks. The chronology of the gun locks, from first use to outmoding, is roughly—matchlock (European), 1470 to 1680; wheel lock, 1510 to 1700; flintlock, 1575 to 1825; percussion cap, 1815 to 1875. It should be remembered that no one knows who invented these locks, nor exactly when nor where. We are not even sure who invented the percussion cap. We do know the percussion cap was developed as a result of Reverend Alexander Forsyth's bringing out in 1807 his detonator lock—the most important development in guns since gunpowder.

'˜. Group of polearms/ Joseph Kindig, Jr. collection.

There are sub classes of each main type of lock. There are a dozen or more distinct varieties of flint locks, including Baltic, snaphaunce, miquelet, Scottish. Knowledge of varieties enables the student better to place a gun in its niche of time.

The halberd with the matchlock—to get back to the illustration —is very rare. The shank of the halberd is hollow and forms the barrel of the pistol. The long spiked end, shown separated from the halberd, is an extension of the shank. The square hole in the blade is intended to receive and hold this pointed end when the end is disconnected.

The polearm with the two wheel locks is a boar spear. Two sets of triggers are provided. One set is near the spear head; the other set is well back on the staff.

The flint piece with the odd forked spear head has the trigger placed about two feet back from the lock.

The percussion cap polearm with the bayonet-like spear has no conventional hand-operated trigger. The gun is designed to fire on impact. Pressure on the point of the bayonet pushes back the trigger to permit the hammer to drive down and detonate the cap.

The year 1836, believed to be the date of manufacture of the double-action Colt revolver pictured in illustration 18, was a momentous one in the field of United States patents, and particularly eventful as far as patented American firearms are concerned. A very disastrous fire in the Patent Office left little known of patents granted between 1790 and 1836, beyond the patentee's name, the year of the patent and the class of invention.

In the United States prior to 1836 very few patents were taken out on guns. About the only guns patented before 1836 of which a few examples have survived are the pistols with the Hart pill locks, invented in 1827.

In 1836 there were two patents issued for revolvers with mechanically turned cylinders. One was the famous "Revolving Pistol" marked PATENT ARMS M'G CO. PATERSON, N. J. COLT'S PT. The other was that champion rarity, the "Rotary Pistol" marked B. AND B. M. DARLING. Both are single-action with cylinders turned mechanically.

The Colt shown in figure 18 is one of several different experimental combination weapons produced by Colt. The blade is noteworthy because of its size, but the most unusual feature of

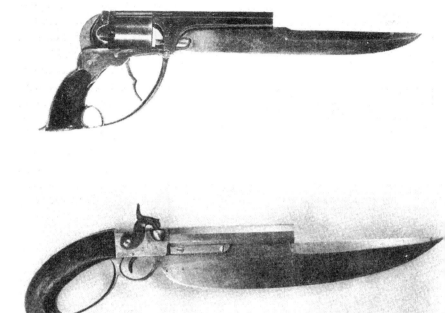

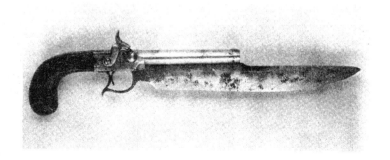

18. Colt revolver/ Colt's Manufacturing Company collection.

19. and 20. Elgin pistols/ Sam E. Smith collection.
      Photographs 19 and 20 courtesy *The Gun Collector*.

the gun is that it is double-action. A strong point about the percussion cap Colt revolvers was the sturdiness of their single-action locks. Mr. Colt was able to use this piece to demonstrate the superiority of the single-action over the double-action.

The combination pistols most sought by American collectors are the Elgin pistols, usually known as cutlass pistols. Mr. George Elgin, of whose history before and after the year 1837 almost nothing is known, obtained U. S. Patent #254, dated July 5, 1837, for "a new and useful instrument called the Pistol-Knife or Pistol-Cutlass". The drawing refers to the "instrument" as a "Pistol-Sword." In the patent specification Mr. Elgin states "The nature of my invention consists in combining the pistol and Bowie knife, or the pistol and cutlass, ..." The blades on the Elgin pistols which I have seen, or of which I have seen photographs, all follow the same pattern as regards the shape of the pointed end. They come closer in appearance to true Bowie knife blades than to conventional cutlass blades.

Charles Winthrop Sawyer listed the Elgin pistol among "arms used by militia, privateersmen, or other citizen martial bodies" and stated regarding it, "The expected sale was to the government to issue to sappers and miners, and to the navy for repelling boarders, and to the merchant marine trading in the Far East, for the same purpose."

Collectors have been uncertain that Elgin pistols, other than two samples, were ever ordered by, delivered to, or paid for by the Department of the Navy. An abridged copy of a letter was published several years ago and was referred to as a contract between Elgin and the Navy. The published reproduction was of an incomplete copy of the original letter. As the copy gave no evidence that the terms of the proposal contained in the letter were satisfactory to the unnamed addressee, students have been aware it was not demonstrated that Elgin pistols should be given martial status.

Now, original documents recently examined, all found in the National Archives Building, Washington, not only tell of the negotiations for the purchase of one hundred fifty of the pistols for the South Seas Exploring Expedition, but also show approval by the then Secretary of the Navy for payment in full for an invoice for the entire number. To me, proof is conclusive that the pistols were not only ordered by, but delivered to the Navy.

It seems advisable to quote at some length from a few of the records of the Department of the Navy, and to give data that will enable any student to locate the original documents.

Here is the story.

In Account Book No. 3, among the records of the Commissioners of the Navy for the period from 1833 to 1842, there is a ledger account for George Elgin which mentions "2 Pistol Knives or Cutlasses made as a pattern—to be left in the Navy Comm's Off." This ledger item, approved by Isaac Chauncey, President of the Board of Navy Commissioners, shows these two pistols cost $20.00 each.

The reference for the next quoted document is—Records of the Department of the Navy: Naval Records Collection of the Office of Naval Records and Library: Exploring Expedition Letters, Volume 4, letter dated September 8, 1837, R. G. 45. The document is a proposal submitted in the form of a letter by Elgin, addressed to "Com. Thos ap C. Jones, U. S. Navy." Jones was at the time a captain and in command of the South Seas Exploring Expedition. The letter reads:

New York 8th Sept. 1837

"Sir:

I propose to furnish for the use of the South Sea Exploring expedition One Hundred & Fifty Pistol Knives of the following description. The form of the Stock or handled (*sic*) to be of the same shape as that of the sample now exhibited but larger, and suitable for a large hand.

The Lock to be of the best materials and workmanship, the Cock of the same to be on the side of the Pistol as usual.

The Barrel to be five inches long made of the Best Steel or Iron either of solid or otherwise as may be directed and to carry forty two balls to the pound which is understood to be of the same size of the modern Navy pistol.

The Blade to be of the best sheer steel eleven inches long forming a Guard over the hand of good temper.

The Blade & Barrel to be Combined by tonge (*sic*) and groove in the best manner either as the sample now furnished or the samples now in the Navy Commissioners office in Washington City.

The Scabbard to be made of leather of the same description as those made by Mr. N. P. Ames for the Ordnance department.

The whole to be tested in the usual manner of testing arms for the Army and Navy of the United States by any officer of the Army or Navy of the U. States or other persons that you may select.

I will deliver them in the City of New York on the 25th day of October Proximo at Seventeen 50/100 dollars each including all the aforesaid appurtenances.

Yours Respectfully,
Geo. Elgin"

Subjoined to the letter are the following notations.

Referring to paragraph 3—"It is agreed that the barrels are to be made of metal that may be most approved by the Superintendent of the Springfield Armory."

Referring to paragraph 5—"It is agreed that they are to be combined in the sam (sic) way as those in the Navy Commissioners office at this time."

Referring to paragraph 6—"Tipped with German silver with a button."

Inserted after paragraph 6—"It is understood and agreed that three extra Nipples or Cones are to be furnished with each pistol and one Wrench to each ten pistols also that the barrels are to be an Octagon and further there is to be a ramrod encased in the scabbard of each pistol."

Below Mr. Elgin's signature is the following subscript:

"Payment to be made on delivery accompanied by satisfactory evidence of proof according to the ordnance regulations of the United States War Department

New York Sept. 8th 1837

(Signed) Thos ap Catesby Jones
Comdg. S.S. Expedition"

The aforementioned Volume 4 of the Exploring Expedition Letters, which, incidentally, is marked "Dec. 1837—Aug. 1838", also contains two other pertinent letters, one dated March 12, 1838, and the other March 27, 1838.

The March 12th letter was from Leverett and Thomas, of New York, to Levi Woodbury. Levi Woodbury was Secretary of the Treasury at the time, and according to Longworth's New York City Directory for 1837 Josiah S. Leverett and Edward I. Thomas were operating a hardware business at 13 Broad Street. In their letter Leverett and Thomas stated they acted as agents for

George Elgin and requested payment in the amount of $2631 for 150 Pistol Knives which had been inspected and accepted by the Navy Yard at Brooklyn. They mentioned they were sending "certificate of inspection"—apparently with the letter.

The March 27, 1838, letter was addressed to "The Honrl. Mahlon Dickerson, Sec. of the Navy" and was signed "Your Obd Svt—Thos ap Catesby Jones, Late Comdr. of S. S. & Expl. Expedition." (Lieutenant Wilkes had succeeded Captain Jones in command.) The letter was in reply to the Secretary's "letter of the 15 Inst. enclosing the bill of Leverett and Thomas." Captain Jones stated the original delivery date of October 25th had been extended to November 15th, but that Elgin had not reported the pistols were ready for inspection until November 20th. Captain Jones then stated he wrote Elgin on November 24th, "It is proper for me to observe that the 15 day of November being the termination of the *extended time* in which by your contract you were to have delivered the articles, it is not impossible that some difficulty may grow out of your non compliance—never will with me if the Pistols are delivered before we sail but should their delivery be *tendered* to another person I think you would meet with some trouble." Captain Jones then went on to tell Secretary Dickerson of "the unquestionable superiority of the weapon over any other for arming Boats crews and exploring parties for penetrating into the interior of Islands inhabited by savages." He concluded his long letter with a recommendation that the bill, less a small incorrect charge for boxing, be paid, "as the arms are well approved of by the Inspection officer and they are in time for the expedition which I understand has not yet sailed."

The reference for the finalizing document is—Records of the Department of the Navy: Naval Records Collection of the Office of Naval Records and Library: General Letter Book # 24, Page 370, R. G. 45. This entry is the original record of the letter written March 30, 1838, to Leverett & Thomas, New York, and reads,

"Gentlemen:
Your bill for 150 Pistol Knives for the exploring Expedition, Amounting to $2631-00 has been transmitted to James K. Paulding, Esq. Navy Agent at New York with directions to pay this amount.
I am, Very respectfully yr Obd
Mahlon Dickerson"

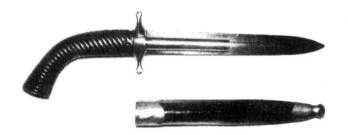

21. Elgin pistol/ Sam E. Smith collection.

22. Elgin pistol/ Henry M. Stewart collection.

23. Dagger pistol/ Frank R. Horner collection.

Secretary Dickerson allowed the charge for boxing—it appears to have been $6.00.

It is still not known whether or not any of these pistols were actually taken on the expedition. Many items that were supplied for use of the squadron were not embarked after Wilkes was put in command. An article in Issue 33 of *The Gun Collector* refers to "5 Bowie Knife pistols—percussion" as being in an 1852 "list of arms at the New York Navy Yard which are not now called for by the regulations."

All Elgin pistols conforming to the specifications approved by Captain Jones and supplied to the Brooklyn Navy Yard were undoubtedly made by Cyrus Bullard Allen, of Springfield, Massachusetts. One such pistol is shown in illustration 19. This is marked on top of the 5" octagon barrel, ELGIN'S PATENT PM CBA 1837, and on the frame, C. B. ALLEN SPRINGFIELD, MASS. It bears the serial #149 and is .54 caliber smoothbore. Notice the most distinguishing feature of this Allen Navy pistol, the unusual hand guard.

Other Elgin pistols, without the hand guards, were made by Allen, and also by Morrill, Mosman & Blair, Amherst, Massachusetts, and by the latter's successor Morrill & Blair. By 1840 all manufacturers of Elgin pistols were out of business.

One of the Morrill, Mosman & Blair pistols bearing serial #13 is shown in illustration 20. This has a 4" round smoothbore barrel and is .36 caliber. Illustration 21 is of a pistol marked MORRILL & BLAIR, AMHERST, MASS. with serial #8. This has a 3" round rifled barrel, .34 caliber. A rare variation of a Morrill, Mosman & Blair pistol is shown in figure 22. In place of the usual back strap this has straps on the sides. It has a 4¼" round rifled barrel, .36 caliber.

No two Elgin pistols are quite alike and no attempt is made here to describe all the variations of size and construction. For such data the reader is referred to *The Gun Collector*, Issue 30, which contains illustrations and detailed descriptions of twenty-odd Elgin pistols.

Illustration 23 shows along with its sheath, a two-barrel knife pistol, one barrel on each side of the blade. The two percussion cap locks have unusual hammers, fired by a single folding trigger. When the blade is sheathed, the hammers seem to be simply

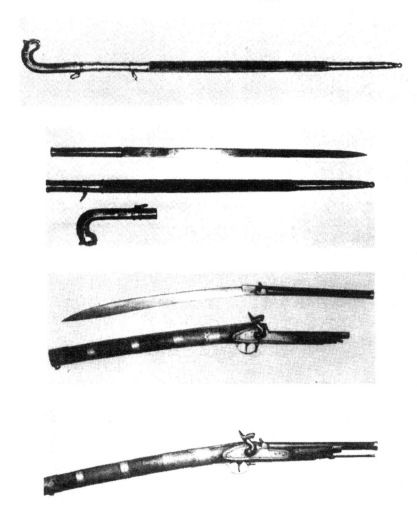

24. and 25. Two views of sword gun/ Eddie Reider collection.

26. and 27. Two views of another sword gun/ Eddie Reider collection.

cross guards, or quillons, and the weapon nothing more than a dagger with a curved handle. The use of a single trigger to fire first the right and then the left barrel was well known in the days of muzzle loading percussion cap guns, but had little popularity except for the superposed load abnormalities which will be discussed in Chapter 9.

Two views, figures 24 and 25, are shown of an eccentric weapon of unknown provenience and indeterminable age. When assembled, the piece resembles a rolled umbrella fitted with carrying rings. There is a velvet covered brass scabbard and a curved brass handle that is easily removed to permit drawing the sword. The steel grip of the sword is a small muzzle loading cannon, fired the same way cannon have been fired for more than 500 years, by touching a lighted match to a primed vent.

The unsheathed product of Burma in figure 26 is somewhat similar to the unsheathed weapon just shown, but the assembled weapon, shown in figure 27, is of more efficient construction. The ease with which the gun barrel may be securely fixed in the gun stock by simply slipping the blade into the scabbard is surprising. There are no screws or other fastenings used or needed to hold the barrel ready for firing. After firing, it is necessary only to raise the percussion cap hammer and give a quick tug on the barrel to release the blade. The barrel makes a sword handle of such length the sword may be swung either with one hand or two hands.

Illustration 28 is of a large combination knife-revolver, or cutlass-revolver, similar to the one being carried by Mr. Daly, as shown in the frontispiece. The revolver is a Belgian 12 mm, 6-shot pin fire, serial 7349, with the barrel built as part of the 12" blade.

A combination of a revolver with a saber, blade scabbarded, is shown in illustration 29. This revolver also is a double-action pin fire. An unusual feature is the construction of the loading gate so it may be set to act as a safety. This piece has no maker's mark, but it has Birmingham proofs.

The sword combination illustrated in figure 30 is the patent model. A few of these weapons were probably produced and marketed commercially. Patent 34,740 was granted March 25, 1862 to Robert J. Colvin, Lancaster, Pennsylvania, for this "Pistol

28. Knife revolver/ Sam E. Smith collection.

29. Saber revolver/ Eddie Reider collection.

Sword". The revolving pistol is a percussion cap model with double-action lock and cylinder automatically turned by the trigger shown inside the sword hilt. The ramrod is held by the attachment at the middle of the scabbard.

Mr. Colvin secured another patent, 44,784, on October 25, 1864, for an extraordinary combination of revolver and bayonet. This probably was never put in production. A copy of the patent drawing is shown in illustration 31.

This is a triple threat weapon. Mr. Colvin states his invention can be attached to any gun and he says, "The gun being fired, the pistol is then operated, and afterward the bayonet can be used." The patent has expired and any one may now make as many of these guns as he wishes. Just put in a second trigger and attach it to a rod so it will fire a revolver that is attached to a bayonet that fits over the barrel muzzle. If complications develop, I suggest the reading of Mr. Colvin's patent specifications —and see if that helps.

Inventions of firearms naturally increase greatly when war comes or threatens. Many patents are granted for arms that die a-borning. These range from meritorious and valuable inventions that are overlooked, to the absurd and bizarre.

The remaining illustrations in this chapter are of patents for combination weapons which if marketed at all, sold in very small numbers.

The combination piece, illustration 32, was not invented under the stress of war. Several examples are believed to exist, but none is available for illustration. R. W. Andrews, the inventor, was given his patent, #328, in July, 1837. In the patent drawing, "A" and "B" show the two parts of the weapon. The stock, the lock, and the knife are in one part; the barrel and the scabbard form the other part. The pistol is made whole by simply pushing the blade home in the scabbard. There are two triggers, one for firing, the other for releasing a catch so the two parts may be disengaged. "If an antagonist seizes hold of the barrel and scabbard, for the purpose of wresting the weapon from the hand of the holder . . . he . . . leaves in the hand of his adversary an unsheathed dagger . . . ready for his destruction"—to quote the patent specification.

Another 1837 patent was that granted to Robert B. Lawton,

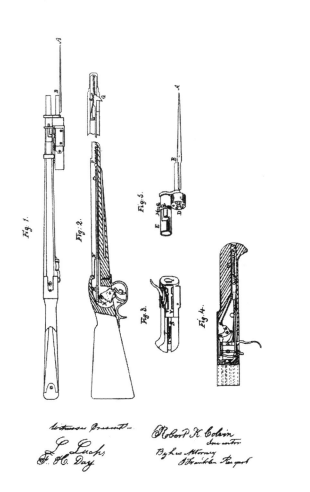

30. Colvin Pistol-Sword/ Smithsonian Institution collection.

31. Colvin Revolver-Bayonet patent drawing.

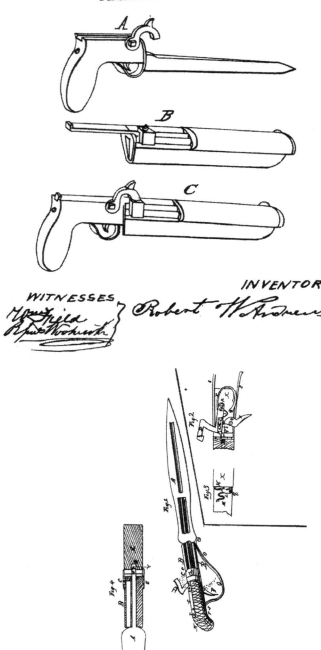

32. Andrews pistol-sword patent drawing.
33. Lawton pistol saber patent drawing.

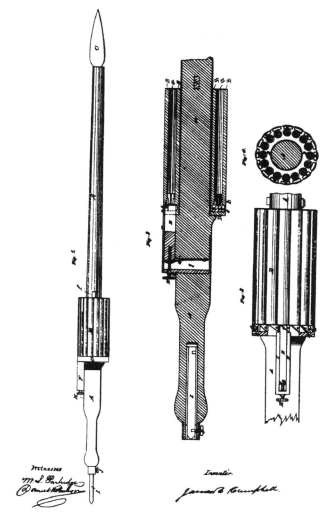

A D 1877 Dec.7. N° 464-4.
DAVIS' Provisional Specification.

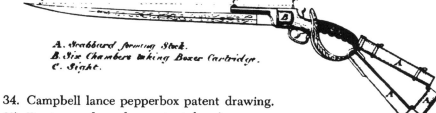

A. *Scabbard forming Stock.*
B. *Six Chambers taking Boxer Cartridge.*
C. *Sight.*

34. Campbell lance pepperbox patent drawing.
35. Davis sword-revolver patent drawing.

of Newport, Rhode Island, on November 23rd, patent #481. As the patent drawing shows, illustration 33, the cylinder revolved around the shank of the blade. Pulling back the trigger turned the cylinder to bring a nipple under the hammer, which was simultaneously raised by the trigger pull. To fire the cocked gun the trigger was pressed forward. To fire another barrel the pulling back and the pressing forward was repeated.

A patent of Civil War days was #39032, granted James C. Campbell, of New York City, June 30, 1863. The patent drawing, reproduced in figure 34, is of a sixteen-barrel pepperbox turning on the shaft of a lance. At close quarters, with the lance leveled at an enemy, this could have been a fearsome weapon, capable of very rapid fire if it functioned as planned. "With the cylinder grasped in the left hand and the back part of the pole in the right hand" a one-sixteenth revolution of the cylinder fired a charge. This manual turning resulted in the edges of teeth at the rear of the cylinder pushing back a hammer against spring pressure. It was assumed when one of the teeth cleared the nose of the hammer, the hammer would be driven forward quickly enough and hard enough to hit and detonate the percussion cap.

The patent drawing reproduced in illustration 35 is of a weapon for which Walter Davis received a British patent, provisional only, #4644, December 7, 1877. In addition to combining a regulation sword with a conventional revolver, Mr. Davis hit on the idea of having the scabbard, cut in sections and provided with stop hinges, to fold up in the form of a rifle stock and to be attached by "a simple slot and catch" to the sword hilt. It should be noticed that the front sight is the tip of the sword.

Chapter 2

MINIATURE FIREARMS

THE DIMINUTIVE has almost universal appeal. In all times expert craftsmen have delighted in making tiny pieces of furniture, incredibly small silver sets, minute musical instruments and working models of machines. Artists with imagination and taste have conceived and executed miniature masterpieces of paintings, books, sculpture.

Before the machine age, the most skilled artisans were employed in making and embellishing armor and weapons. The miniature firearms that have been produced by handwork, with consummate skill, infinite patience and with much artistic talent, have always been collected and treasured by connoisseurs.

Collectors are not in agreement as to just what a miniature firearm is or how small it must be. Some will include such small but still full-size pieces as Kolibri automatics and Gem revolvers. Others will consider any small-scale reproduction a miniature, and perhaps they will be joined by all students of semantics. Still other collectors will say a miniature firearm must be so small it can not be held in normal fashion in even a baby's hand. This last concept will be generally followed in this chapter, but some models of modern pistols illustrated may not meet the "baby's hand" requirement.

There are modern firearms miniatures of excellent craftsmanship. Examples will be pictured in this chapter. None of the recently produced—since World War II—"watch charm" cartridge pistols made in quantity in several foreign countries will be illustrated. Those cheaply made pieces are not regarded as collector items.

41

Painstaking effort was more commonly found in earlier and less hurried times—so most of the illustrations will be of old pieces. Photographs can not do justice to these old and tiny firearms. The art in one of the old miniatures can hardly be realized to the full until a fine "small and beautifully less" model is held in the hand.

Color photography helps to better appreciation. Of the miniatures, illustration 36, from The Metropolitan Museum of Art collection, which are shown here in black and white, six are shown in color on the front of the July, 1949, *American Rifleman*, and described in the *Rifleman's* accompanying article written by Stephen V. Grancsay.

The eight pieces in illustration 36 are of different types and range in size from just under two inches to a shade over four inches in length. They vary in quality of workmanship, but all are in operating condition. The four at the top are German all-metal wheel locks made in the late 1500's, of steel and brass, showing engraving and mercury gilding. The two ball butt German dags, perhaps slightly later, are of steel and wood, with one having the wood inlaid with ivory. At lowest left is a miquelet pistol and at lowest right a miquelet blunderbuss. The pistol is very unusual and may have been made by a German gunsmith as an experimental model probably early in the 17th century. The stock is of copper, engraved and mercury gilded, and is of wheel lock type. The lock, of steel, is a miquelet with South Italian characteristics. The blunderbuss miniature is a Spanish piece of a little later date, gracefully shaped. It has a wood stock with lock and furniture of steel. The capucine and the belled part of the steel barrel are of brass.

An exceptional group is shown in figure 37. The miniatures go from a very modern German drilling back through percussion cap, flintlock, miquelet, to wheel lock. At the top of the uncased pistols is a very fine all-metal piece with a beautifully executed miquelet lock. The copper hue of the frame, the bright steel of the lock, the intense blue of the barrel, combine to make this outstanding. This piece is 4¼" overall.

Below the miquelet pistol is a ball butt all-metal wheel lock pistol, and below that is a miniature wheel lock arquebus. The latter includes in the engraving on the stock figures of animals

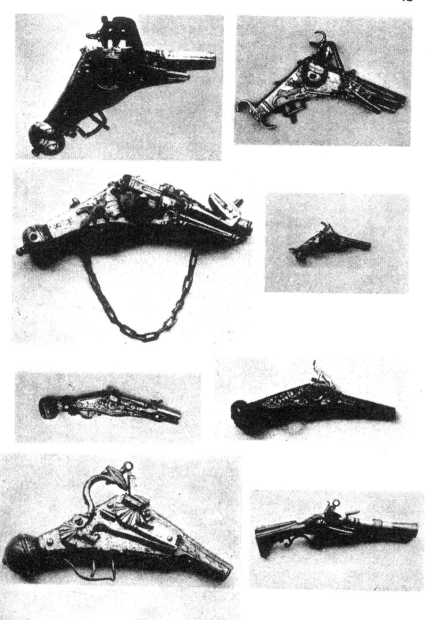

36. Group of miniatures/ Metropolitan Museum of Art collection.

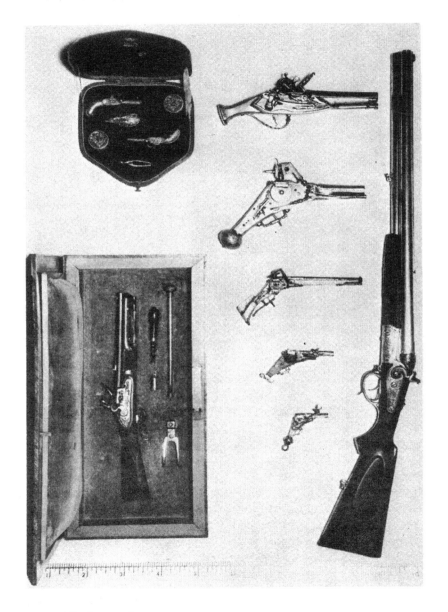

37. Group of miniatures/ Dr. W. R. Funderburg collection.

and of a man carrying a gun. Below the arquebus are two wheel lock pistols, one 2¹⁄₁₆", the other 1⁵⁄₁₆" overall.

The pair of percussion cap pistols, complete with accessories, is contained in a fitted case of red leather. The grips of the pistols, the flask, the round bullet and cap containers, are of gold nicely engraved.

The cased flintlock rifle has a stock of finely figured wood, delicately carved. The furniture is of silver, finely engraved. The boar engraved on the trigger guard is very realistic. The octagonal rifled barrel has PETER AUER IN BURGLENGENFELD cut in script.

There seems to be a dearth of working flintlock miniatures, and a complete absence, as far as I can find, of snaphaunce miniatures.

The German drilling, which has two shotgun barrels with a rifle barrel underneath, is as finely made as any of the guns made by the early craftsmen. All the distinctive features that set drillings apart from other multishot guns are faithfully copied in miniature in this model. You may be sure the folding rifle sight on the barrel rib will rise automatically when the lever back of the hammers is pushed forward so the right hammer will fire the cartridge in the rifle barrel. The checkering on the pistol grip and on the fore end is very fine. The engraving on the furniture is of particular interest because of its great delicacy. Screw heads on full size guns of this type are customarily engraved. They are engraved on this model.

On plate 38 there is another illustration of this drilling, taken down and in its case. The wooden case has an elaborately carved panel on the top, with insets of ivory and ebony.

The other illustrations on this plate are of contemporaneous miniatures of pocket pistols and revolvers of the nineteenth century. All the revolvers shown are six-shot. The revolver alone in the odd shaped leather case has pearl grips and uses rim-fire cartridges, six of which are shown below a rammer which fits in a separate compartment of the case. The three other revolvers have ivory grips and use pin-fire cartridges. The revolver with the pair of pistols has a case of ebony, gold inlaid. The case directly below is of gold-inlaid onyx. The pistols in it are of steel and gold. So are the pistols at the bottom right, in a case of

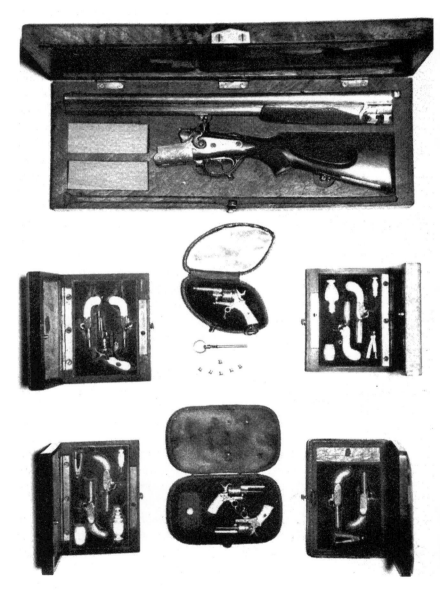

38. Group of miniatures/ Dr. W. R. Funderburg collection.

tortoise shell fitted for one accessory only. This accessory is a combination bullet mold, barrel wrench and nipple wrench. The case at the middle right is lustrous pearl. The pistols and revolvers in these cases vary only $\frac{1}{8}''$ in length, each being between $1\frac{5}{8}''$ and $1\frac{3}{4}''$ overall.

Of the very small miniatures of firearms probably the most minute of working models were made by Mr. G. M. Sibbald of Leeds, England. From the 1880's to the 1930's Mr. Sibbald made working models of engines, carriages, bicycles and locks, as well as guns, with parts so small they may well be called microscopic. A gold bicycle, weighing $\frac{1}{4}$ ounce, has 292 distinct parts: a lock about $\frac{1}{8}''$ square and weighing less than $\frac{3}{4}$ grain, has 12 parts. (I use the present tense advisedly, because these and the other Sibbald pieces now exist in the collection of Robert Abels of New York City.)

"The Smallest Show on Earth", as Mr. Sibbald chose to call his collection, was widely exhibited in England for a space of fifty years. Many press clippings of the time gave generous space to praise of the rare pieces, telling of medals awarded, mentioning special exhibitions by Royal Command before Queen Victoria at Windsor Castle and The Princess of Wales at Sandringham, and speculating as to whether any one else had eyesight equal to Mr. Sibbald's. Mr. Sibbald worked without the aid of a glass.

The five pieces illustrated in figure 39 are believed to be the entire production by Mr. Sibbald of miniature guns. It is hoped their tiny dimensions will be emphasized by the two Ford car keys in the illustration.

The one inch gold revolver, encased in an almond shell weighs 35 grains and has 76 parts.

The two pistols, gold with ivory grips, just below the revolver are in a plum stone. Each weighs $6\frac{1}{2}$ grains and is made of 19 pieces, or parts. The barrels of these two single-shot pistols turn to the side to load.

One of the two little gold pistols at the bottom of the picture has two barrels that tip up to load, is made of 36 pieces and is of 15 grains weight. The other of the two, a single-shot, is made of 19 pieces and weighs 9 grains.

It is hardly believable but it is true that the two hammers on this extraordinary double barrel pistol are made to drop alter-

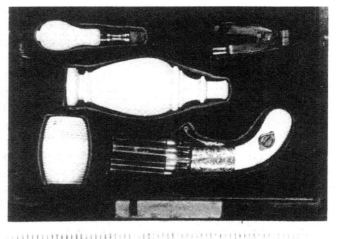

39. Group of miniatures/ Robert Abels collection.

40. Miniature pepperbox/ Dr. W. R. Funderburg collection.

nately. When both hammers are cocked, the first trigger pull will let down only the right hammer, but a second pull will let down the left hammer.

The cased pepperbox, figure 40, does not have the extremely small dimensions of the Sibbald pieces, but it is still very small, and it goes to the top of the class as a work of art that functions perfectly. The one-inch scale in the illustration shows the gun to be 2⅛" overall. The gun can be fired just like a full size 6-shot Mariette pepperbox. The typical screw barrels are revolved by the double-action lock which turns the cylinder and raises and drops the hammer with one pull of the trigger. The accessories include an ivory powder flask, an ivory barrel for caps, an ivory-handled screw driver, and a combined mold, barrel wrench and nipple wrench.

Miniatures and small scale models are illustrated, plate 41, surrounding a full-size Remington double-barrel derringer. The primary reason for showing this full-grown Remington is to indicate the comparative sizes of the other pieces, but the gun itself warrants more than just passing mention. It is not only presentation engraved with beautifully engraved sterling grips—it is one of the rare Remington over-and-unders with automatic ejector and in caliber .44 long.

The five small scale Remingtons on the plate are—the two double derringers in the middle, the 1871 U. S. Army at top left, the 1866 U. S. Navy at the top right, the vest pocket derringer at bottom left. Also at the bottom is a case containing a pair of percussion cap pistols, complete with accessories, and an old single-shot pin-fire pistol. Then there is a Hopkins & Allen pistol on a reduced scale, with a miniature pin-fire revolver and a miniature Japanese matchlock pistol above it. On the right, below another much engraved pin-fire revolver is a modern autoloading pistol, and below the latter is an antique wheel lock pistol. The Colt Walker and the Colt Paterson are huge in comparison with the Sibbald miniatures, but they are accepted as miniatures by nearly all gun collectors.

If any gun collector exists so benighted he does not know which of the Colts is the Walker, let me say that another Walker, on a more reduced scale, is the gun under the Yale key in plate 42. At the top, in plate 42, is a pair of concealed trigger, percus-

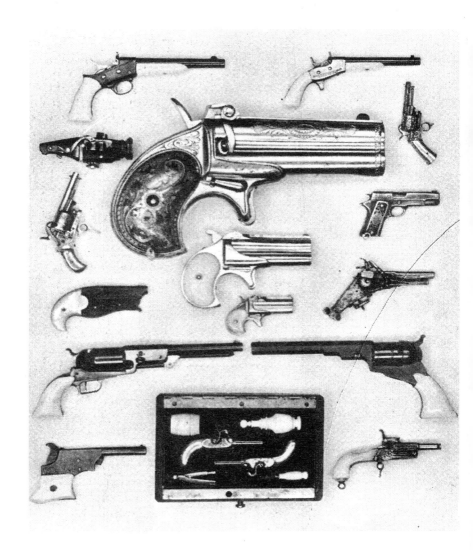

41. Group of miniatures/ Harry C. Knode collection.

42. Group of miniatures/ Robert Abels collection.

sion cap pistols, in a case with accessories. Below the Walker is a finely engraved precision made miniature of a .45 Colt autoloading pistol, in working order and complete with a magazine clip. This is not cheap, though being made of gold it is economical, as it does not require polishing—as some one said about gold bathroom fixtures. An old watch charm pistol of gold is below the Colts. On the side is an accurately made and fully working model of an 1898 Mauser, once a regulation German Army rifle.

At the top of plate 43 is a pair of engraved top hammer, folding trigger, percussion cap pistols in a leather case measuring about 3¼" x 2¼" x ¾". The accessories are well proportioned and complete. In one corner of the case is a velvet covered compartment for bullets.

Below the cased set is a French six-shot double-action revolver with blued frame and pearl grips. The revolver can fire the six rim-fire bulleted cartridges, if the fulminate in the little cartridges be sufficiently fresh to explode.

At the bottom of plate 43 are two very interesting miniatures. The one at the left which looks like a revolver is actually the scarce watch charm pistol patented by Samuel Dosick of Providence, Rhode Island, on May 12, 1931, United States patent #1,805,080. There are hardly any external, and only minor internal, differences between this Dosick pistol and the pistol patented March 3, 1931, United States patent #1,794,364, by L. S. Chilson of Attleboro, Massachusetts. Both are single-action pin-fires, with tip-down barrels, almost identical in appearance. Mr. Chilson assigned his patent to J. M. Fisher Company, of Attleboro, and it seems that most of the American pistols of this type were "Fisher Firesure".

Mr. Chilson named his invention a "Toy Pistol"; Mr. Dosick named his a "Pistol Charm"! It may not be irrelevant to point out that the thoughtful applicant for a patent gives careful consideration to the name to give his invention. In an instance like this does he wish his patent application studied by an examiner of toys, of firearms, or of jewelry?

The little pistol on the right just below the Yale key is an English folding trigger percussion cap pistol, 2¼" overall, and of about .12 caliber. The finely checkered wood grip has an inset silver name plate. The plate is not inscribed but the gun itself is engraved JOSEPH CHILD, presumably the name of the maker. This gun not only can be, but has been, fired. The barrel bears the Birmingham markings proving it was test fired.

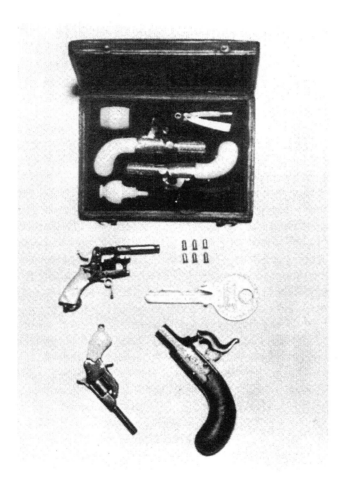

43. Miniatures—Cased pair, Harold Berger collection—Revolver, Mrs. Albert Foster collection—Two pistols, Arnott J. Millett collection.

Chapter 3

TWO-BARREL REVOLVERS

WE ARE ACCUSTOMED to thinking of a revolver as a weapon with one cylinder containing a number of chambers, usually five or six, firing one shot from each chamber through a single barrel. Most are like that, but revolvers have been made, some in considerable quantity, equipped with two barrels, or with two cylinders, or designed to fire two shots from a single chamber. Such revolvers may be classed as curiosa.

In this chapter we shall consider those revolvers which deviate from usual form in that they have two barrels.

Though guns with two barrels, and revolvers with one barrel, were known in the days of flintlock and even wheel lock ignition it is improbable that any revolver with two barrels was constructed until after Forsyth invented the detonators. I do not know of any two-barrel revolvers made before those manufactured by Billinghurst. William Billinghurst, of Rochester, New York, was in his day the maker of the finest guns produced in this country. His double rifles and revolving rifles were eagerly bought by wealthy sportsmen of South America and India, and his products were the only American firearms conceded equality with the British "best" guns.

Billinghurst made the two-barrel gun illustrated in figure 44. The novel features of this gun were not patented. Mr. Billinghurst took out no patents on any of the various unusual firearms he made. The gun is a combination of a 7-shot rifle and a shotgun, using pill-lock ignition. In place of a conventional solid

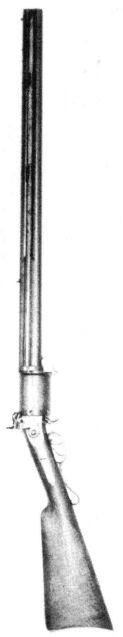

44. Billinghurst rifle-shotgun.

center pin there is a shot barrel upon which the cylinder revolves. This substitution of a shot barrel for the center pin was later a claim in the patent granted Dr. Alexandre Le Mat.

The 7-chambered cylinder for the rifle is turned manually and keeps the proper chamber in alignment with the barrel by use of a perfectly fitted catch under the barrel. A close examination of this cylinder makes us better understand the high praise accorded Billinghurst workmanship by the connoisseurs of fine guns. In this cylinder the chambers are rifled to match the barrel rifling.

The lock is single action with two separate hammers and triggers. The rear trigger is connected with the hammer that fires the bullet loads in the cylinder. To fire the shot barrel the under-hammer is cocked and the forward trigger pressed.

It has been thought the Billinghurst gun gave Le Mat the idea for the latter's revolver. The Le Mat revolver employs a cylinder revolving around a shot barrel but has an entirely different lock mechanism.

Some collectors incline to the belief Le Mat revolvers were manufactured, beyond the experimental stage, in the United States. Mr. Tom McHugh, who has done much research on Le Mats, is very doubtful that there are American Le Mats. In *Firearms of the Confederacy,* by Steuart and Fuller, it is stated there is no evidence Le Mat revolvers were manufactured in this country.

That certain revolvers, because they are either unmarked, or not marked as being made in Europe, should be classed as American Le Mats is an unjustified assumption. The fact a New Orleans newspaper at the outbreak of the Civil War stated that manufacture for the Confederacy of Dr. Le Mat's "grapeshot revolver" was "contemplated" is not evidence any Le Mats were made in the United States. After that published report it is unlikely Dr. Le Mat had sufficient time to fulfill any plans for manufacture here before he left for France, in 1861, to arrange for production there.

Much less study has been given the man and his titles than has been given his revolvers and where they were made. In various New Orleans directories from 1851 to 1859 are found, progressively, "Dr. A. Lemat, 188 Dauphine St.", "Dr. R. Le Mat, 188 Dauphine St.", "Dr. R. Le Mat, 124 St. Peter", "Dr. A. Le

Mat, 215 Bourbon". On his 1856 patent his name appears as "Dr. Alexandre Le Mat"; on his 1869 patent it is "Francois Alexandre Le Mat" with no title given. Mr. HcHugh has found no record that Le Mat was a member of any medical association of the period, but feels Le Mat's claim to "Doctor" is much stronger than his claim to "Colonel". Mr. McHugh was unable to find the inventor's name on the roster of any military organization before, during or after the Civil War.

Most Le Mats were made on the continent of Europe. Usually those guns have "Paris" included in the barrel markings. All not made on the continent were probably manufactured in England.

The patent for the percussion Le Mat was granted Dr. Alexandre Le Mat, October 21, 1856, U. S. Patent #15925. There were only two claims in the patent: one was for the substitution of a shot barrel for the usual solid center pin; the other was for a "gun-cock with a double hammer". Actually, Dr. Le Mat offered two ideas for the construction of a cock that would "explode at pleasure" either a cylinder cap or the center barrel cap. One idea was the use of a one-piece cock with two fixed hammer noses, but with a percussion cap for the shot barrel held in a sliding bar. With the slide out, the top hammer nose was free to strike caps on the cylinder nipples; with the slide pushed in the lower hammer nose could fire the shot barrel while the top nose could not reach a cylinder cap. The other idea was for a two-piece hammer with a movable nose that could be depressed for the firing of the lower, or center, barrel. Dr. Le Mat stated he preferred the two-piece arrangement. The Le Mats we find today in collections will nearly if not quite all be of this type.

One Le Mat may possibly differ from another not at all, or only in some single detail, but the chances are the next Le Mat you see will be different in several ways from the last one you saw. Two percussion Le Mats are pictured in figures 45 and 46. Each fires nine bullets through the upper barrel and a buckshot charge through the lower barrel. One has a full octagon barrel, the loading lever on the left, a set screw to keep the top barrel in position, and an oval trigger guard. The other has a part octagon, part round barrel, the loading lever on the right, a spring catch to hold the top barrel, and a spur trigger guard. There are other minor differences, in the loading levers, in the movable hammer noses, and in the lanyard ring fastenings. The

revolver with the octagon barrel has Paris markings; the other
has no marking other than "Col. Le Mat's Patent" on the
barrel.

The Le Mats had fire-power—nine shots from the cylinder
as against the usual six, and in addition there was that heavy
buckshot charge that must have been a sure man-stopper at
close quarters. Except that none of the various types of hinged
nose hammers is sturdy, and that the loading levers are not of
as good design as the levers on the best American revolvers of
the period, the percussion Le Mats are of fine construction. The
odd caliber, .40, of the bullet used in Le Mats was not desirable
at a time most Army revolvers were .44 caliber. Those Le Mats
that came through the blockade brought high prices in the Confederacy. Le Mats were carried by such famous Southern leaders
as General Beauregard and General Stuart.

After the War, on December 14, 1869, U. S. patent #97780
was granted "Francois Alexandre Le Mat, of New Orleans", for
a breech-loading two-barrel revolver designed to use center-fire
metallic cartridges. The patent specifications indicate that in
this revolver Le Mat contemplated the firing of a conical ball
in the large center barrel.

Illustrations 47 and 48 are of two center-fire Le Mats.

On these breechloaders the hinged hammer is of improved
but still fragile and not standardized design. There are two gates
in the breech, one to permit insertion of cartridges in the cylinder, the other to permit loading a cartridge in the lower barrel.
There is a rod for ejection one at a time of cartridges in the cylinder. There is also a mechanism for extracting the cartridge in
the center barrel. This goes in operation automatically when the
loading gate is opened. The larger of these revolvers, figure 47,
is stamped "2", presumably a serial number, and is like the
patent drawing in all respects apparently. This is marked "Colonel Le Mat, Paris." The cylinder, being only 1⅛" long, takes a
very short cartridge, of about .45 caliber. The lower barrel takes
a cartridge of about .60 caliber. The short barrel Le Mat, figure
48, serial #30, uses cartridges of about .38 caliber in the cylinder
and .50 caliber in the lower barrel. Minor differences in construction of the two guns may be noticed. For instance, in the
case of the small gun the beak is put in position to fire the lower
barrel by pressing down the thumb piece on the hammer,

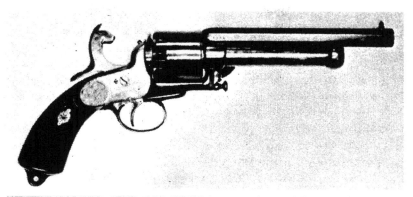

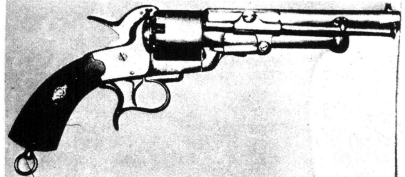

45. Le Mat cap lock.

46. Le Mat cap lock—14" overall/ Glode M. Requa collection.

47. Le Mat center-fire/ Joseph W. Desserich collection.

whereas on the larger revolver the thumb piece is pressed up.

The percussion and center-fire Le Mats pictured here all have top barrels rifled, and center barrels smooth. One of the pin-fires illustrated has both barrels rifled. Pin-fire Le Mats were probably made in large numbers in Europe, but their export to this country was small. The use of pin-fire cartridges was always thought risky here, and their transportation by common carrier was severely restricted. The revolvers called pin-fire Le Mats regularly used pin-fire cartridges, commonly 12 mm, in the cylinders, but percussion cap ignition in the center barrels, which were usually about .60 caliber. Illustration 49 is of such a pin-fire Le Mat, marked "Colonel A. Le Mat Brevete" and bearing Belgian proof marks, serial 3023. Illustration 50 is of a pin-fire Le Mat that uses 9 mm cartridges in the cylinder and has a rifled barrel of about .45 caliber. This lacks the Belgian proofs.

Though all the Le Mats illustrated here have 9-shot cylinders, some center-fire and some pin-fire Le Mats were made with 10-shot cylinders.

Le Mat revolvers were also made in long guns. They have shoulder stocks and long barrels and are bigger and heavier in every way, but otherwise there are no decided changes in construction. Though none is illustrated here the collector should not overlook the fact that Le Mat long guns are scarcer and harder to find than Le Mat short guns.

Illustration #51 is of a percussion cap revolver that is notably different from Le Mats and other two-barrel revolvers. The two barrels in this revolver, bored in a single block, are neither side-by-side nor superposed; they have "one bore on one side and below the other". The two concentric rows of chambers in the cylinder have axial nipples for the outer row and oblique nipples for the inner row. There are two hammers, operated by a single trigger, with the right hammer having a square nose to hit the axial nipples in the outer row, and with the left hammer having a slanting nose to insure striking squarely the caps on the obliquely set nipples. These unusual features are evident in the patent drawing, reproduced in illustration #52. The patent, #35404, was granted Aaron C. Vaughan, of Bedford, Pennsylvania, May 27, 1862.

Notice also in this Vaughan revolver the unique hinged loading lever designed to ram charges in two adjacent chambers simultaneously.

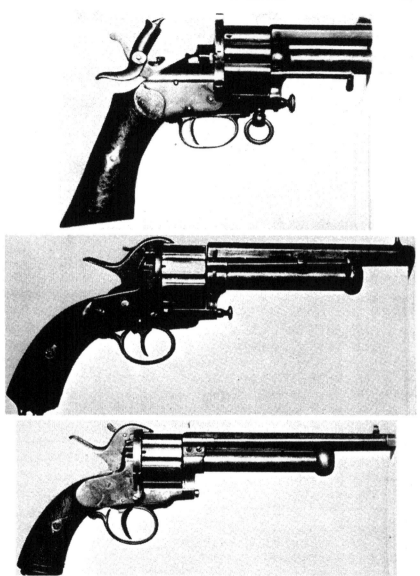

48. Le Mat center-fire/ Joseph W. Desserich collection.

49. Le Mat pin-fire—12" overall/ Joseph W. Desserich collection.

50. Le Mat pin-fire/ Joseph W. Desserich collection.

The cylinder is rotated when the two hammers are cocked simultaneously. Pressure on the trigger drops the right hammer; a second pressure drops the left hammer.

The following year Mr. H. D. Ward of Pittsfield, Massachusetts, obtained a patent for a two-barrel metallic cartridge revolver with barrels side by side. This was patent #39,850, granted September 8, 1863. Illustration #53 is a reproduction of the patent drawing. Figure 3 in the drawing shows the muzzles of the lateral barrels. In this Ward revolver, which like the just described Vaughan has two hammers and one trigger, the unusual feature is the choice of operation given the user. He may fire one shot at a time, operating the gun like a conventional single-action revolver, cocking the hammer and pulling the trigger for each shot, or he may discharge two shots "without recocking between the discharges". Further, these two shots, one through each barrel, may be "either in such rapid succession that the discharge seems to be simultaneous or with an intermission of any desirable interval between the discharges."

To fire the gun as conventional revolvers are fired, use is made of the right hammer only. To fire the double shots without recocking, both hammers are cocked at the same time. Then when the trigger is pulled the right hammer falls first, but if the trigger is "pulled directly back the whole distance at once" the two shots are in unison. If the trigger is pulled "until the first hammer is felt to escape, and then allowed to rest for a time" the firing of the second shot may be delayed or even forgone. The two-at-a-time shots may be repeated by cocking both hammers simultaneously. Obviously, the cylinder must have an even number of chambers. The illustration shows eight.

Of the two-barrel revolvers the most dubious as to practicality of construction and the most controversial as to provenience is the Albert Christ. There are only a few of these guns in existence, and where they were made is uncertain. The U. S. patent, #57864, dated September 11, 1866, was taken out by "Albert Christ, of California, Hamilton County, Ohio". The Christ revolver, illustrated in figure 54, is an 18-shot cartridge revolver with two superposed barrels. The chambers, for .22 caliber rimfire cartridges, are in two concentric circles in the cylinder, twelve being in the outer row and six in the inner. The hammer has a single, small unadjustable nose which strikes always at the

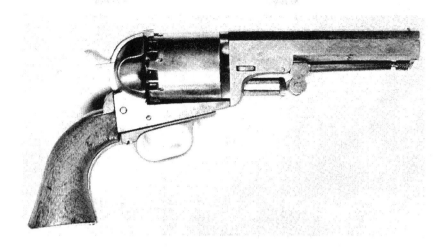

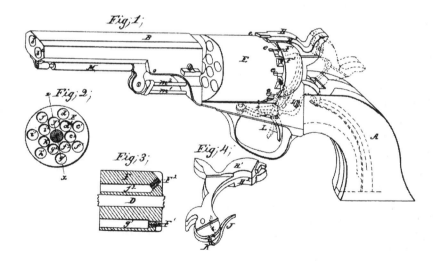

51. Vaughan revolver/ Smithsonian Institution collection.

52. Vaughan revolver patent drawing.

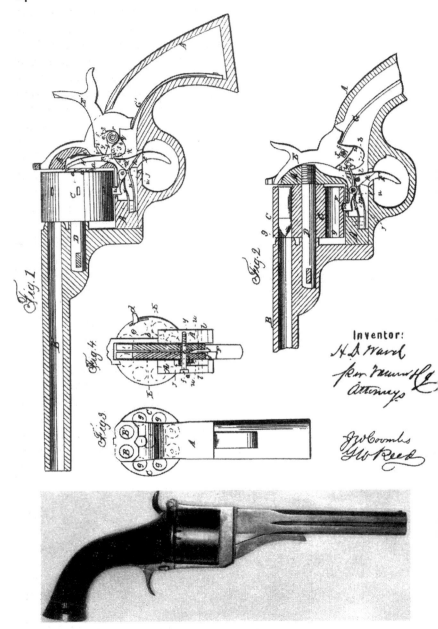

53. Ward revolver patent drawing.

54. Christ revolver/ Osborne Klavestad collection.

same distance from the periphery of the cylinder. After striking in succession the rims of two cartridges in the outer circle the striker must hit the rim of a cartridge in the inner circle. This requires uncomfortably close fitting of the two concentric rows of chambers. The rotation of the cylinder is accomplished by two "feed-fingers", moved by cocking the hammer. These "feed-fingers" do not turn the cylinder by pressure against teeth of a ratchet; they turn it by pressure directly against the rims of the cartridges. These radical features are found in no other revolver.

In the firearms field Rollin White was one of our most prolific inventors. One patent granted him in 1855, which he sold to Smith & Wesson, probably caused more furore and frustation and law suits among arms manufacturers than any other patent before or since. The many other patents granted Mr. White caused no particular commotion. The one for a two-barrel revolver, #100,227 of February 22, 1870, raised not a ripple.

The peculiar revolvers made under this 1870 patent are among the scarcest of American revolvers, but they were not successful, and what is more important, their patent did not stop manufacture of other revolvers of conventional type.

In his patent specifications Mr. White tried to cover all contingencies. He claimed the supplemental barrel whether placed "above, beneath, at the side of" the regular barrel, "so that it is arranged in front" of the cylinder. He claimed further the supplemental barrel when not in front of the cylinder, provided it was "above the cylinder and ordinary barrel". The patent drawing includes an illustration showing an auxiliary barrel placed above the regular revolver barrel and extending over the cylinder. In this case the hammer has a movable beak. Another illustration in the patent drawing has the auxiliary barrel hinged in front of the cylinder, to drop down and away from the revolver barrel. Firing of the lower barrel was by means of a firing pin working through the center pin, or by a firing pin fixed in a sliding center pin. The construction might be such that the charge in the auxiliary barrel could be fired with the first shot from the cylinder, or such that the charges from the two barrels could not be fired simultaneously. Certainly, very few of the possible permutations were ever utilized.

Each of the two Rollin White revolvers illustrated in figures 55 and 56 fires seven .22 cartridges through the upper barrel and

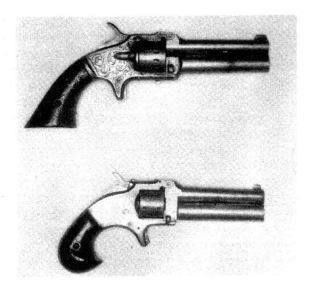

55. Two Rollin White revolvers/ Osborne Klavestad collection.

56. Another view of the same revolvers.

one .41 cartridge through the lower auxiliary or supplemental barrel. On these illustrated guns the auxiliary barrels turn for loading as shown in the second illustration. The upper barrels tip up for cylinder loading. On one gun the lower barrel turns end for end, perhaps with the Perry & Goddard "Double Header" idea of having fired cases ejected by the next shot from the reversed barrel.

Most revolvers use cartridges all of one size. Mr. White said his invention was designed "to overcome this objection". Mr. Owen Jones of Philadelphia, Pennsylvania, had another idea to permit the use of "projectiles of different sizes in the same revolver". Figure 57 is a reproduction of the drawing in patent #151,882 which Mr. Jones obtained June 9, 1874. Notice the barrel block has two bores of different sizes. Notice also the cylinder in the butt. There are two cylinders furnished with bores corresponding to the two barrel bores. With the small bore cylinder in firing position the barrel with the corresponding bore is placed uppermost. Depressing two spring latches permits changing the cylinders and also turning the barrel group, thereby making the large bore of the changed cylinder coincide with the large bore barrel.

Still another two-barrel revolver designed to shoot cartridges of two calibers is the "Osgood Duplex". This revolver was patented December 7, 1880, patent #235,240, by Freeman W. Hood, Norwich, Connecticut. The example shown in illustration 58 is marked only "Duplex" with the patent date. That is the usual marking. Sometimes the marking includes "Osgood Gun Works, Norwich, Conn." Examples have been reported marked "Monarch". This single-action cartridge revolver has its two barrels made in one piece which is hinged at the bottom. Raising the catch in the upper part of the frame permits tipping down the barrel block and sliding the cylinder off the extension of the lower barrel for loading or unloading. There is no ejector. The hammer has a movable nose, similar to that on the Le Mat, but the lower barrel is not fast to the standing breech, as it is on the Le Mat. The cylinder holds eight .22 short cartridges which fire through the upper barrel. The center barrel holds one .32 cartridge.

Illustrations 59 and 60 are of two French double-action pin-fire revolvers. Each has two barrels and two concentric rows of chambers in its cylinder. Figure 59 shows a gun marked "Le

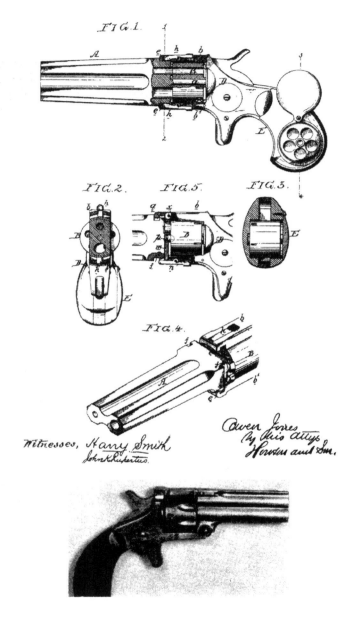

57. O. Jones patent drawing.

58. Osgood Duplex revolver.

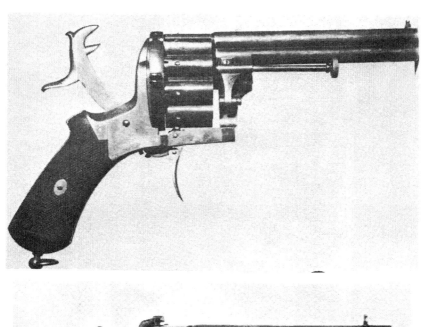

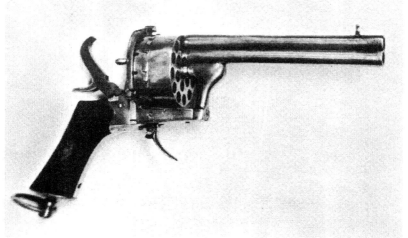

59. 20-shot revolver—10" overall/ George N. Hyatt collection.

60. 18-shot revolver/ Governor Gordon Persons collection.

Page Freres a Paris". This is a 20-shot, with ten chambers for 7 mm cartridges in each row. By means of the two fixed beaks on the hammers shots are fired alternately from the two rows. The gun has on the right a loading gate and also an ejector which is swivelled to take care of expulsion of fired cases from both rows of chambers.

The other pin fire, figure 60, is an unmarked 18-shot, firing twelve 7 mm cartridges from the outer ring of chambers and six from the inner ring. The hammer has only one striking nose, but there is a sliding member in the standing breech which rises when the hammer is cocked and falls with the fall of the hammer. This sliding piece, which fires the cartridges by driving in their pins, has two steps arranged so that one shot from the inner ring of cartridges through the lower barrel follows two shots from the outer ring through the upper barrel.

Illustration 61 is of a finely made, modern European two-barrel double-action revolver. The cylinder holds sixteen .32 S & W center fire cartridges in two concentric rows of eight each. The two sturdy strikers are integral with the hammer. The chambers are so spaced that though both strikers descend together only one cartridge can be fired at a time. Chambers in the outer and inner row fire alternately. The gun, hinged at the top, opens at the bottom when a spring release is pressed. A manual ejector extracts all sixteen cases together. When pressure is released from the trigger the hammer automatically comes back a small fraction of an inch, to keep the striker free of the cartridge primers.

A German "Bar" pistol is shown in illustration 62. Guns like this had wide sale and could be bought from dealers in modern weapons until quite recently. The cartridge block is a rectangular prism holding four .25 A. C. P. cartridges. As the shells lie over one another the construction permits a very flat weapon, easy to conceal. The firing pin moves back and forth to fire the barrels alternately. After the trigger has been pulled twice, a catch on top of the pistol is pressed and the cartridge holder turned through 180 degrees, so that the two remaining shells are in firing position.

61. 16-shot revolver—9″ overall/ Arnott J. Millett collection.

62. "Bar" pistol.

Chapter 4

TWO-CYLINDER REVOLVERS

LET'S HAVE IT CLEAR that the term "two-cylinder revolver" as used here refers to a revolver having two cylinders which are both installed on the same center pin whenever the revolver is fired. The term does not apply to a revolver with a center pin that will hold either of two cylinders, but which will not hold both cylinders at the same time.

In the early days of metallic cartridges several gun makers produced successful revolvers that would detonate either the new cartridge primers or the old percussion caps, and for such revolvers supplied an extra cylinder. Those guns were reasonable and successful. The revolvers designed to use two, or even more, cylinders at the same time, were unbelievable and unsuccessful.

Though four of the illustrations for this chapter are taken from photographs of patent models now on display at the Smithsonian Institution in Washington, it is not to be assumed, and it is not true that these oddities were so completely unsuccessful that none but the patent model was made of any. Recently there still existed at least one each of Sneider, Philip, and Linberg & Phillips revolvers that were not patent models. Ray Riling showed me a Philip and a picture of a Linberg & Phillips.

I found record of patents granted for only five of these freaks. I intend to give no detailed description of any. I will take them in turn according to their patent dates, and mention briefly only how each is supposed to be fired.

On March 18, 1862, United States patent #34,703 was granted

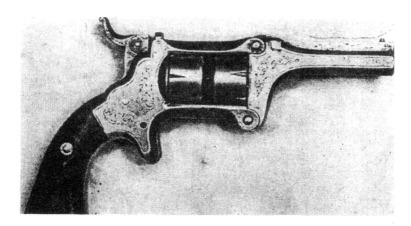

63. Sneider revolver/ Photograph courtesy Montclair Public Library.

64. Gardner revolver/ Smithsonian Institution collection.

65. Linberg & Phillips/ Smithsonian Institution collection.

C. E. Sneider for a revolver, illustration 63, with two 7-shot cylinders chambering small caliber rim-fire cartridges. The two cylinders were alike and were arranged breech to breech on a center pin having both ends alike. The cartridges in the forward cylinder pointed toward the revolver muzzle; those in the other cylinder pointed toward the shooter. A long hammer struck the rims of the cartridges in the forward cylinder. When those cartridges were all discharged, the cylinder pin was turned around so the unfired cartridges in the other cylinder would come under the hammer. The gun was hinged at the bottom to permit dropping the barrel so the cylinders could be reversed.

On May 16, 1865, United States patent #47,712 was granted to G. H. Gardner for a revolver, illustration 64, with two percussion cap cylinders, the forward one 5-shot, and the rear 6-shot. The front cylinder had a sixth chamber, but that was bored clear through and served only as a rearward extension of the barrel to guide bullets fired from the rear cylinder. The two cylinders could be hooked together, so they would rotate together and so the caps in the front cylinder would be exploded by a slide driven forward over the rear cylinder when hit by the hammer. When the bored through chamber came in line with this slide the front cylinder could be uncoupled and would cease to revolve though the rear cylinder would continue to revolve when the hammer was cocked. A falling hammer would now strike a cap in the rear cylinder and the bullet would pass through the front cylinder and on through the barrel.

On December 6, 1870, United States patent #109,914 was granted Charles Linberg and William Phillips for a revolver, illustration 65, with two identical 6-shot cylinders, that could be shifted on the center pin, for alternate use. A cylinder placed in the front revolved as the hammer was cocked; when placed in the rear it could not turn. A small longitudinal boring between two chambers contained a firing pin. With a cylinder locked in the rear position, its firing pin received the hammer blow and transmitted it to a cap, or primer, in the cylinder in front. (The chambers were provided with screwed-in nipples that could be removed to permit use of metal cartridges. A chamber in the front cylinder when in line with the barrel was of course always in line with the firing pin, or needle, rather than with a chamber in the rear cylinder.) In the fully loaded Linberg & Phillips gun the bullets in the rear cylinder pointed toward the shooter, as did those in the previously described Sneider, figure 63. When the front cylinder was empty the two cylinders and the center pin were reversed.

On August 26, 1873, United States patent #142,175 was granted W. H. Philip for a metallic cartridge revolver, illustration 66, having two or more cylinders designed to rotate one at a time in succession and so contrived that when one cylinder is empty the cylinder immediately in back will at once be put in motion by the next cocking of the hammer. In the model shown, there are three cylinders. Each has seven chamber borings. In the front cylinder and also in the rear cylinder six borings are recessed to hold cartridges. In the front cylinder one boring is reserved to do service as a portion of the barrel for the middle cylinder; in the rear cylinder one boring is reserved to hold a firing needle. The middle cylinder has five borings recessed for cartridge heads. In this cylinder one boring serves only as a portion of the barrel for the rear cylinder; and one boring holds a firing needle. So, the gun holds seventeen cartridges.

When the front cylinder has been revolved by a pawl following grooves in the cylinder until its reserved open chamber is in line with the barrel, the pawl then moves into a groove in the middle cylinder and turns it until its reserved open chamber,——etc., etc. The cartridges in the rearmost cylinder are struck by direct blows of the hammer; those in the middle cylinder are struck indirectly by blows of the hammer on the firing pin contained in the rear cylinder; those in the front cylinder by blows of the firing pin contained in the middle cylinder when that pin is driven forward by the pin in the rear cylinder, when that pin is hit by the hammer. All clear? I am glad there are no more cylinders.

To reload the cylinders and get them not only in proper sequence but with their chambers readjusted—let's not go into that.

On March 17, 1874, United States patent #148,742 was granted to W. Orr for a metallic cartridge revolver, illustration 67, having two 6-chambered cylinders and a hammer with two striking noses. One nose, at the forward end of the long hammer, reaches over the rear cylinder to strike the cartridges in the front cylinder. The other nose, located at the rear of the hammer and missing from the patent model here illustrated, is a short pointed screw running through the hammer. This has a knurled screw head which permits the striking end being adjusted so it will either strike or fail to reach a cartridge in the rear cylinder.

One of the six chambers in the front cylinder is reserved for use as a portion of the barrel for the rear cylinder. Therefore, the gun is an 11-shot revolver.

With the adjustable striking nose in the rear of the hammer screwed back so it will not reach the cartridges in the rear cylinder, the five shots from the front cylinder are fired. During the firing of these five shots the front cylinder revolves with the rear cylinder. When the reserved open chamber in the front cylinder comes in line with the barrel the front cylinder ceases to revolve. Now the adjustable firing pin is screwed in and the six shots may be fired from the rear cylinder.

Many possible questions about these remarkable two-cylinder guns are here left unanswered. If any reader needs to know how cylinders were removed, or how a cylinder could be either turned or prevented from turning, he may get the inventor's answer by studying a copy of the appropriate patent paper, a soft copy of which may be had—25¢ each at this time—from the Commissioner of Patents, Patent Office, Washington, D. C.

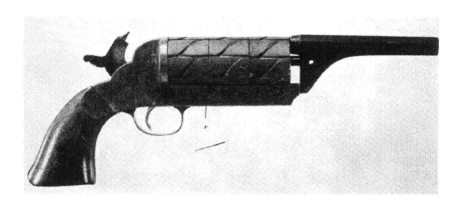

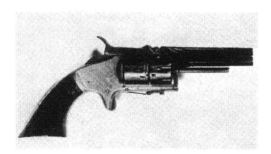

66. Philip revolver/ Smithsonian Institution collection.

67. Orr revolver/ Smithsonian Institution collection.

Chapter 5

SQUEEZERS AND
KNUCKLEDUSTERS

A SQUEEZER PISTOL is not held in normal fashion to be fired by the squeeze of a finger on a conventional trigger. It is held in the palm and fired by tightening the fist. It is often called a palm pistol.

The best known of the squeezers is the "Protector Revolver". Illustration 68 is a reproduction of an advertisement that appeared in the Hartley & Graham 1892 catalogue. If the reader of today doubts the statement in the advertisement that the "Protector" could have been carried in the vest pocket as easily as a watch, he forgets the 18-size Waltham Vanguard, which I believe was the smallest watch railroad engineers and conductors were permitted to carry in the 1890's. The 1894 catalogue of Hartley & Graham shows the same gun in the same hand, but the separate illustration of the gun shows the cap with the name "Chicago Fire Arms Co." rather than "Minn. Fire-Arms Co." The 1894 advertisement says the gun is "compact, light, effective, strong, durable, quick, safe, convenient, and reliable." The 1892 advertisement did not state it was convenient.

The "Protector" was patented in the United States, March 6, 1883, by Jacques Turbiaux, Paris, France, patent #273,644. Previously, patents had been granted in France, Belgium, England and Italy. Peter H. Finnegan, Austin, Illinois, was granted a further patent on August 29, 1893, patent #504,154. Usually both patent dates will be found on the American pieces.

The cartridges for a "Protector" were loaded in a turret-like

HARTLEY & GRAHAM.

A New Principle--The "Protector" Revolver.

THE "PROTECTOR."

68. Reproduction from Hartley & Graham 1892 catalogue. Courtesy the Bella C. Landauer Collection, New York Historical Society.

69. Group squeezer pistols/ Frank R. Horner collection.

cylinder to which access could be had by unscrewing a side plate called a cap. The squeezing action revolved the cylinder and drove a firing pin against a cartridge primer.

At the top in figure 69 is a late Chicago Fire Arms Co. model. This has smoked pearl sides, and the safety that is automatically released by finger pressure when the hand grip is squeezed. The Minneapolis Fire-Arms Co. model, the middle one in the illustration, is slightly smaller and has the usual rubber side plates. This has the earlier safety which must be separately released before the gun is fired. Both the American pieces are seven-shot, using short .32 cartridges. The slightly smaller French "Le Protector Revolver de Poche", at the bottom in the illustration, is ten-shot, using a cartridge of smaller caliber. The French wording on a cartridge box furnished by Frank Wheeler indicates these European Turbiaux squeezers were also made in 8 mm, seven-shot.

A late Chicago model fitted with a double-ringed finger guard is shown in figure 70. This unusual supplementary device was made by John T. Norris, Springfield, Ohio. The squeezers supplied by Chicago Fire Arms Co. equipped with Mr. Norris' invention are very scarce and outstanding oddities.

Illustration 71 is a reproduction of a direction sheet glued to the inside of a box in which a Chicago Protector was packed. The name at the bottom, Ames Sword Co., is that of the actual manufacturer. Collectors who exhibit these squeezers and hold them wrong side up, with the middle finger pressing the safety, should notice the injunction in paragraph 2 to use the forefinger. The third paragraph may indicate why a Chicago Protector is so rarely found in proper working order. Paragraph 6 might be shortened to the first four words.

A single-shot squeezer is shown in figure 72. This particular piece bears the patent date of May 2, 1905, and was patented by George Webber, Chicago, patent #788,866. The barrel unscrews to take a .32 center-fire cartridge. The gun is held in the palm of the hand with the hard rubber end resting against the base of the thumb. Pressure by two finger tips against the ring which slides along the barrel cocks the gun. When the ring is drawn fully back the firing pin will be disengaged and driven against the cartridge primer by spring pressure.

Illustration 73 is of a twentieth century .22 caliber Shatuck

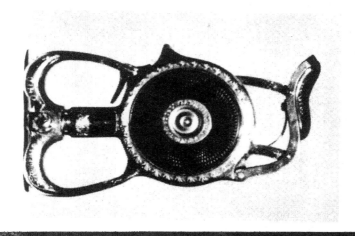

Directions for using the "Protector" Revolver.

1. To Load. Hold the revolver flat with the trigger pointing to the left. Turn the cap with the thumbs or the palm of the hand a quarter turn to the left. Then holding the forefinger on the safety catch turn the pistol over till the cylinder drops out. Load from the center of the cylinder and replace it with the notches down. Replace cap and turn to the right.

2. To Fire. Press the forefinger on the safety catch while you press the trigger with the palm of the hand.

3. Never snap the trigger unless either the revolver is loaded or a leather buffer is placed on the firing pin. After loading remove the leather and replace leather when the firing is discontinued.

4. The cylinder should be kept oiled on both sides and the revolver should be cleaned after firing before being laid aside.

5. Use Winchester Metallic catridges, No. 32 extra short, rim fire.

6. Never snap the pistol without a careful examination whether it is loaded.

Address:

AMES SWORD CO., Chicopee, Mass.

70. Chicago Protector/ Eddie Reider collection.

71. Chicago Protector direction sheet.

Unique, marked UNIQUE C. S. SHATUCK ARMS CO. HATFIELD, MASS.
It was patented December 4, 1906, by Oscar F. Mossberg, Chico-
pee Falls, Massachusetts, patent #837,867. There are four short
barrels bored in a solid steel block which drops for loading when
a vertical catch is released. The gun is gripped in the hand and
fired by squeezing a sliding part which operates a rotating firing
pin. The Shatuck Unique pistols were made in both .22 and .32
caliber, some with iron frames blued and some with iron frames
nickel-plated over an under-plate of copper. Some had horizontal
barrel catches.

Rough copies of the "Unique", probably all made in Europe,
are sometimes found. One imitation, with no maker's name, is
marked INVISIBLE DEFENDER.

Of the European squeezers the best known is the Gaulois. A
nicely engraved example, together with its case, is shown in
figure 74. What appears to be a fine leather cigar case is actually
a case fitted for the pistol and extra cartridges.

The Gaulois is fired by squeezing in the sliding part of the
gun, as a "Protector" is fired. In operation it is different in that
the squeezing and releasing moves a cartridge from the magazine
in the handle, inserts it in the barrel, fires it and then ejects
the case. It reminds one of an automatic, but it does not utilize
the force of recoil in any way, as the automatic does. In the
Gaulois, as in an automatic, the bullet does not have to jump a
gap when fired, as the bullet does in the "Protector" or in other
revolvers when it passes from the cylinder to the barrel. A point
favoring the Gaulois over the revolver is this prevention of gas
leaks, and a point favoring the Gaulois over the automatic is the
fact a defective cartridge in the Gaulois will not hinder the firing
of the next cartridge, since the release of squeezing pressure on
the Gaulois will mechanically throw out the defective cartridge.

Probably most of the Gaulois squeezers were plain, 5-shot,
8 mm models, sold without any carrying case. As the gun is a
shade under ⅝″ thick and would make no unsightly bulge in a
pocket most purchasers probably preferred to do without the
cigar case disguise. The small lever on the side of the frame is a
safety.

In the Gaulois the sliding part rests against the base of the
thumb and is pushed forward in firing. In the Rouchouse, another
French squeezer, the sliding part rests against the fingers and

72. Webber pistol—4" overall/ Robert Abels collection.

73. Shatuck Unique.

74. Gaulois with case/ Frank R. Horner collection.

is drawn back in firing. The Rouchouse, illustration 75, has a barrel that moves back around the cartridge as the sliding part is squeezed.

The Tribuzio, figure 76, is classed by collectors as a squeezer and is probably the most sought of the European repeating pistols of this type. It was invented in 1890 by Catello Tribuzio of Turin, Italy. Like the two French pieces just mentioned, it loads cartridges from the top into a vertical magazine. No clip is used for loading in any of these squeezers. This is an all-metal pistol, operated by the squeeze of the middle finger inserted in the ring.

One of the oddest of squeezers is the LITTLE ALL RIGHT, figure 77, patented by Edward Boardman and Andrew Peavey, both of Lawrence, Massachusetts. Patent #172,243 was granted January 18, 1876. Above the octagon barrel is a round tube with a slot in it for the sliding trigger—called "pull" by the inventors. The inventors' instructions for firing state, "The pistol is held in the palm of the hand, the end of the barrel resting on the second finger, the forefinger being placed around the pull, which should be elevated . . ." Elevating the pull is mentioned because that protruding trigger may be folded down over the muzzle when the gun is not in action. To use the words of the patent, "The pull serves not only as a finger-piece, but also as a guard or stopple to prevent foreign substances from entering the barrel." These 5-shot .22's were regularly supplied with hard rubber grips, marked LITTLE ALL RIGHT, with the patent date, and ALL RIGHT FIRE ARMS CO., MANUFACTURERS, LAWRENCE, MASS. U.S.A.

A squeezer pistol is shaped unconventionally so it may be gripped in the palm when being fired. A knuckleduster pistol is shaped unconventionally so it may be comfortably gripped in the fist for use as a punching or pounding weapon. The knuckleduster is always all-metal.

The best known knuckleduster pistols are the short pepperboxes stamped "My Friend". They were made in 7-shot, .22 caliber; 5-shot, .32 caliber; and 5-shot, .41 caliber. The really scarce ones are in .41 caliber. Probably all .41's have safeties; the other calibers were made both with and without. The one illustrated, figure 78, is a .32 with safety. The old hardware catalogue advertisements regularly offered the .32 in 6-shot, but the .32's were actually 5-shot, like the one illustrated here.

On advice of counsel I now point out regarding squeezer pistols

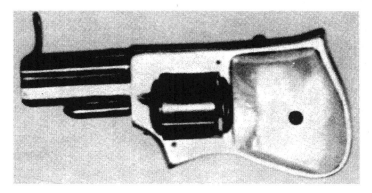

75. Rouchouse pistol—5″ overall/ Anthony A. Fidd collection.
76. Tribuzio pistol/ Frank R. Horner collection.
77. Little All Right/ Governor Gordon Persons collection.

that "Protectors" are nowadays commonly illustrated wrong side up, that Shatuck is usually incorrectly spelled with two "t's", and that Little All Right is sometimes incorrectly referred to as "Little Miss Alright."

Mr. James Reid of Catskill, New York, who was granted patent #51,752 on December 26, 1865, for "My Friend", claimed only the formation of the ring in the all-metal frame and a safety designed to lock the cylinder with the hammer between cartridges. The safety slides in a groove under the frame. When drawn back at a time the hammer is midway between cartridge heads in the revolving cylinder it pushes a stud through an opening in a muzzle shield and into a barrel muzzle, making the cylinder immovable. This type of safety is not feasible with a 6-shot gun, and Mr. Reid noted in his specification that he contemplated only cylinders with an uneven number of barrels.

These short Reid pepperboxes, which are marked on the left above the cylinder, MY FRIEND PATD DEC. 26, 1865, have center pins which "turn wrong". Lack of that knowledge has caused many owners to put undue pressure on the flattened tip of the center pin and to break it. The pin must be removed in order to take out the cylinder for loading or reloading.

Let's go back to the "ring or bow" as Mr. Reid called it. Illustration 79 is a reproduction of the patent drawing which shows the pepperbox "grasped in the hand as a means of defense", with the little finger passed through the "ring or bow."

Of the tales about "My Friend" one story I am inclined to accept is that a Sing Sing keeper—could it have been an inmate? —suggested to Mr. Reid that a better grip for striking a blow could be had by adding a barrel. Anyway, such guns were made by Mr. Reid. Two types of these all-metal 5-shot, .32 caliber revolvers are shown. Figure 80 has a brass frame, 81 a steel frame. The latter, marked REID'S NEW MODEL MY FRIEND, seems less an outgrowth of the pepperbox form than does the brass-frame model. The addition of the barrel may have resulted in the use of a different grasp when "hitting a blow for self-protection", so perhaps "knuckleduster" does not apply to the Sing Sing inspired development of the footpad's companion.

Long before "My Friend" was created another all-metal combination of pepperbox and "knuckler" was made by William & John Rigby, Dublin, Ireland. Illustration 82 is a side view of a

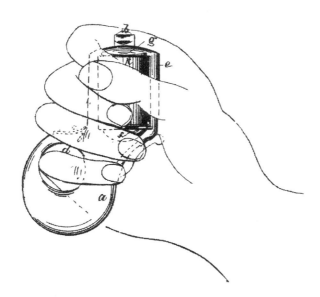

78. Reid's My Friend pepperbox.

79. Reid's patent drawing.

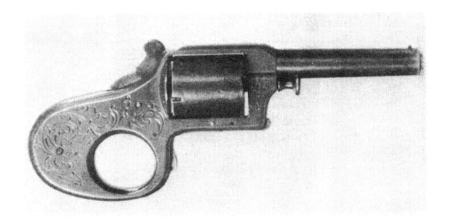

80. Reid's My Friend revolver—7″ overall.

81. Reid's My Friend revolver/ Glode M. Requa collection.

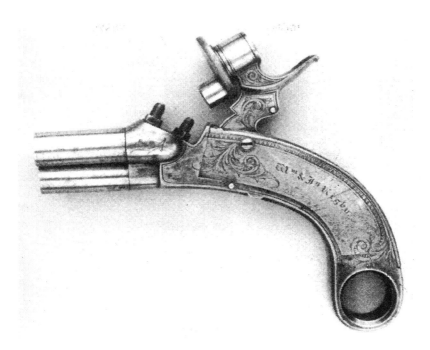

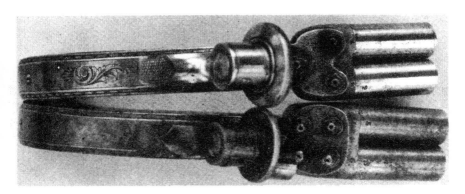

82. Rigby pistol—5¼" overall/ W. Keith Neal collection.

83. Two Rigby pistols/ W. Keith Neal collection.

3-shot; illustration 83 is a top view of both a 3-shot and a 4-shot. I am sure a few were made in 6-shot.

These early Rigby pieces employ a curious percussion cap lock mechanism. The striker is part of a plate that is revolved manually to hit the capped nipples one after another. In addition to the peculiar lock, this Rigby pistol was intentionally designed to serve as a striking weapon, and for that reason it fully qualifies for inclusion in this book. Guns by other British makers were made with lock mechanisms identical with these Rigby locks but as they had conventional wood grips they are arbitrarily omitted. If I admit a gun just because it has a strange lock I open the door to an unmanageable host.

These single-action, folding trigger Rigbys have screw barrels which were numbered to insure each barrel would go back to its own place. The four-barrel gun illustrated has barrels marked 5, 6, 7 and 8—with the breeches similarly marked, of course,— so it appears these guns were made in pairs.

The most sought of the knuckleduster pistols are those triple-threat French weapons which have grips with four finger holds, and which when folded leave no doubt as to how they may be grasped. Two views of one of the so-called Apache Knuckledusters are shown in illustrations 84 and 85. This combination of firearm, dagger and brass "knucks" is marked L. DOLNE INVUR and is supposed to have been popular with Paris apaches, gangs of criminals notorious for violence. The two pictures show how the blade, the handle and the trigger may all be folded. The gun is 6-shot, double-action, and fires a 7 mm pin-fire cartridge.

A more efficient and scarcer type of this weapon is shown in figure 86. This is marked DELHAXHE. On this the only folding part is the blade, which may be turned to lie close up on the inside of the frame. When gripped in the hand as a knuckleduster the Delhaxhe is in shooting position, unlike the Dolne. The forefinger is on the trigger, and if the blade is open the piece is also in position for use as a dagger. The Delhaxhe has a safety, a simple bar which may be caught in the trigger to prevent its movement. An ejecting rod may be seen, screwed into the frame.

The all-metal cartridge derringers, mostly .41 rim-fires, first put out by Moore Patent Fire Arms Co., Brooklyn, then by the National Arms Co., Brooklyn, and lastly by Colt's Patent Fire Arms Manufacturing Co., Hartford, are frequently referred to by

84. and 85. Two views of Dolne pistol/ Eddie Reider collection.

collectors as knuckleduster pistols, and for that reason are included in this chapter. I am not aware that any of the three companies that manufactured this pistol, of which an example is shown in figure 87, ever sanctioned the designation, or even alluded in advertising to the pistol's possible use as a knuckleduster. Mr. Daniel Moore, of Brooklyn, New York, who was granted patent #31,473 on February 19, 1861, went no further than to say the unusual shape gave a more firm grasp in shooting. In explaining the proper grasp he said, "the forefinger takes against the under side of the barrel . . . while the trigger is discharged by the middle finger of the hand."

The piece illustrated, figure 87, was manufactured by Colt and is marked COLT'S PT. F.A. MFG. CO. HARTFORD, CT. U.S.A. Colt bought out the National Arms Co. and presumably all its manufactured stock, about 1870, and used the name "The National Deringer" in advertising the pistol as late as 1888, when the retail price per pair was $7.00. The guns had been made for about five years by National Arms Co., that manufacturer having succeeded Moore Patent Fire Arms Co., who were apparently manufacturing the earliest examples before the granting of the patent in 1861. The earliest of the Moore pistols are marked PATENT APPLIED FOR. Two of the Moore derringers are shown in figure 88, with barrels rotated sideways for loading. The upper, which bears the serial 3840 and the name "Moore", is like the later pieces made by National and Colt, except that it does not have the knife blade cartridge extractor of those later derringers. The lower, which bears serial #37 and PATENT APPLIED FOR, is considerably different. It is like the patent drawing for Daniel Moore's "Breech-Loading Fire-Arm", as it was designated, which was the first cartridge derringer.

It is sometimes difficult to say if a change in construction of an original model results in a new model or merely in a variation— or to decide at just what point in a succession of very minor changes a new model emerges. An improvement in the shape of the hammer or the relocation of a screw may reasonably be considered by the collector as of little importance and not constituting a model change. The two Moore derringers can hardly be classed as variants of a single model—the differences are too marked and too numerous. Most important, the early one is made for a center-fire cartridge. The patent drawing clearly depicts the

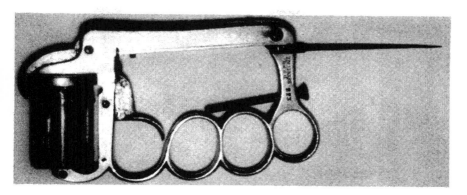

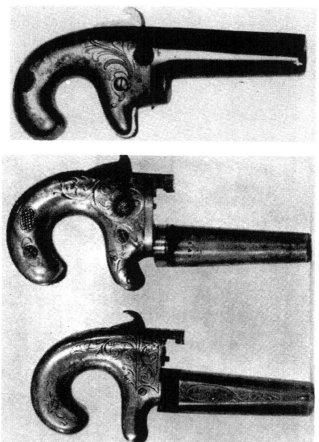

86. Delhaxhe pistol/ Dr. W. R. Funderburg collection.
87. Colt #1 Derringer/ Colt's Manufacturing Company collection.
88. Two Moore Derringers.

hammer nose as striking a center-fire cartridge, but no description of the cartridge, much less a specimen of the cartridge itself, is known to exist. The center-fire piece has a straight rather than curved trigger housing, and the barrel release button on the left instead of the right. The barrel turns down to the right for loading, whereas the barrel on the later rim-fire turns to the left.

A collection of all-metal knuckleduster pistols would not be large, but it would be difficult to complete. The .41 My Friend is scarce; the center-fire Moore and the 6-shot Rigby are very scarce.

Chapter 6

ALARM AND TRAP GUNS

AN ALARM GUN, when it explodes its powder charge, announces to any one in hearing that it has been disturbed. Usually it does nothing more than sound an alert, though it may start a bell ringing, or even provide a little light by scratching a match.

A trap gun that fires a powder charge announces not only it has been disturbed, but that it has fired a shot at its disturber. The disturber may be an animal, or it may be a human intruder. Some of the trap guns, such as the North & Couch and the Reuthe, designed solely to shoot foraging small game, were almost sure to get dead center hits. The poacher-shooting trap guns were less dependable.

Most alarm guns are intended to warn against intrusion, but not all. Among exceptions is the sundial gun which simply announces the arrival of noon. A good example of one of these scarce pieces is shown in figure 89. This has a stone base about nine inches in diameter and a gun about six inches long. The gun, when properly set up in the north-south line, is designed to fire a saluting charge at apparent noon. It differs from other small muzzle-loading cannon in having a long trough-like and powder filled touch hole running parallel with the bore. With the dial's gnomon, more often called "the thing", set in the plane of the meridian the sun's rays will pass through the burning glass at noon, focus on and ignite the powder. As the sun at noon is higher in summer than in winter, the burning glass is made to be adjustable through an arc in the plane of the gnomon, so

95

89. Sundial gun/ Robert Abels collection.

90. Knight and Dragon alarm/ Joseph Kindig, Jr. collection.

the sun's rays will cross the powder trail. The gun is also capable of similar movement.

The gun shown can be set up to fire at noon anywhere but it will properly mark time only if set up at the correct latitude and longitude for which the time lines were cut on its face. Sun clocks of almost split second accuracy have been made, but the dial made for Middletown will not "work" in Centerville.

It is thought the first wheel lock was invented by a German clock maker. Certainly the early clock makers were closely linked with the makers of locks for wheel lock guns. The very extraordinary all-metal piece shown in illustration 90 is operated by clockwork and will fire a wheel lock alarm gun at any appointed hour. After the necessary preparations—loading the gun with a charge of powder, spanning and priming the wheel lock, winding and setting the clock—a lever is set to trip at the desired hour. When the hour hand on the dial reaches and moves the lever a bell starts ringing, the knight's lance strikes the dragon, the gun goes off and a princess emerges through the door in the tower. The action, of course, depicts the old tale of the knight's killing the dragon and rescuing the princess.

The firing of the gun takes place when the knight's right foot comes down. Movement of the foot opens the pan cover and releases the wheel on the lock.

Another alarm, this one French, which fires a 16 gauge pin-fire cartridge by clockwork is shown in illustration 91. The mechanism here is quite like that of the modern kitchen timer. The pointer on the dial is set for the number of hours that are to elapse before the alarm sounds.

The piece is all iron. The striker is the long arm pivoted at one end and with a heavy dog's head at the other. The illustration shows this arm raised slightly past the vertical and resting against a much shorter arm which turns as the hand on the dial moves. When the short arm finally pushes the striker back until the force of gravity takes over, the striker head drops and drives in the cartridge pin. The illustration shows the barrel unloaded, but with the breech swung back to receive a cartridge.

The alarms of the sundial guns and the clockwork guns did not cause the consternation that was felt when the discharge was heard of the flintlock alarm shown in illustration 92. This gun was fitted in a door lock and the discharge told of an attempt

91. Alarm gun—10¾″ overall/ Hampton P. Howell, Jr. collection.

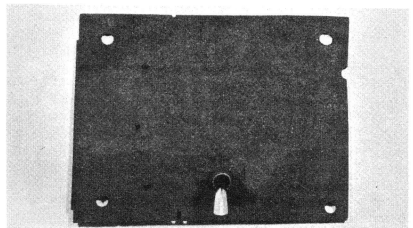

92. Door lock alarm—10″ x 9″/ Photograph courtesy Herb Glass.

at unlawful entry. Some one who did not know the secret of the lock was trying to get in a locked room. The door lock was so peculiarly arranged that the key would turn back the bolt only if given a series of turns in a prescribed order—the first turn being in the "wrong" direction. If the first turn was in the "right" direction the bolt would not move but the gun would fire.

Before the percussion cap was invented few guns were made simply to sound an alarm. The percussion cap brought with it many small and simply made burglar alarms. Nearly all were made to be fastened to a door jamb or window sill, to fire when door or window was opened. When the door or window moved it tripped a spring-backed hammer which exploded a cap. The invention of the small rim-fire and pin-fire cartridges brought out quantities of even more simply made burglar alarms, which operated essentially the same as the percussion cap alarms.

The two little burglar alarms in figure 93, which shoot .22 blanks, are probably the ultimate in simplicity. The two are alike, but one is shown set for use and the other in fired position. The one at the left has its hammer held by a protruding bit of metal, while the one at the right has had its hammer nudged aside so the cartridge held in the rounded end of the metal plate has been struck quite violently. These devices sold at wholesale for a dollar a dozen.

The next dozen illustrations will be of other alarms, some percussion cap and some cartridge, which operate much on the same principle and of which descriptions will be brief.

Number 94, patented by Simeon Coon, Ithaca, New York, September 22, 1857, patent #18,236, is probably the best known. In this the spring, which is shown resting on the nipple in the fired position, is itself the hammer. The 1872 Great Western Gun Works catalogue advertised this at a price of $3.00, with caps at 15 cents per hundred.

Figure 95 shows another earlier Coon alarm. This was patented by David Coon, Ithaca, New York, May 26, 1857, patent #17,406. The patent was assigned to B. F. Chesebrough, whose name appears on this example. It has a sharp pin in addition to a screw to help fix the gun in position. The barrel itself is thrown down by spring pressure, so its capped nipple will hit an unmoving hammer.

The alarm for which Noah Chaffee, Athens, Pennsylvania, was

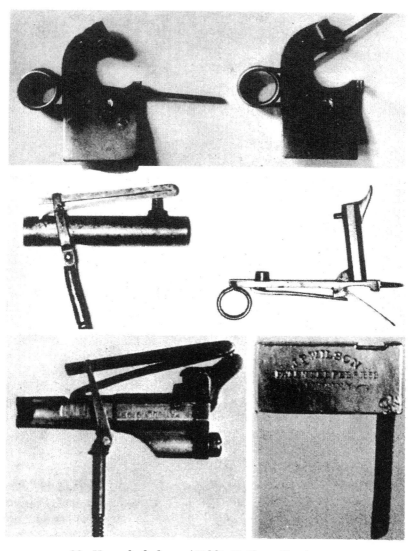

93. Unmarked alarms/ Eddie Reider collection.

94. S. Coon alarm/ Anthony A. Fidd collection.

95. D. Coon alarm/ Eddie Reider collection.

96. Chaffee alarm/ Anthony A. Fidd collection.

97. Wilson alarm/ Anthony A. Fidd collection.

granted U. S. patent #542,407 on July 9, 1895, and which is illustrated in figure 96, seems to be the Simeon Coon alarm adapted for use with .22 rim-fire cartridges. This is shown with the combined hammer and mainspring just coming in contact with a pivoted striker whose sharp end will explode a cartridge. The loose linking of the spring-hammer to the gimlet screw is the same on both the Coon and the Chaffee alarms. It is evident a moving door or window pushed very lightly against the hammer will drive it down.

The very compact brass alarm, shown in figure 97, was patented February 8, 1859, U. S. patent #22,911, and bears the name "J. P. Wilson", with the patent date. The patent was granted jointly to Mr. J. P. Wilson and to Mr. John F. Thomas, the latter being known to us as the inventor of the Remington cane gun. This alarm is an ingenious quick-demountable affair. The dovetailed slot provides a snug fit for the head of a special gimlet screw—not shown—which is screwed into a door casing when the gun is in use. The barrel and the nipple are both concealed in the body of the alarm. When the striking arm is down and resting on the nipple the gun measures about 1¾″ x 1″ x ½″.

The figure 98 brass alarm is the old Wilson alarm converted to cartridge, with a slightly different screw attachment. There is a small pin on the pivoted arm, to fire a .22 short. This piece is unmarked. The cardboard box in which it was packed was marked "The American Portable Burglar Alarm". The printed price was $1.00.

The little alarm marked REIFF & MC DOWELL, PAT. JUNE 13, 1893, PHILADA PA., shown in figure 99, seems to be another adaptation to cartridge of the Wilson & Thomas product of 1859, shown in figure 97. This piece lacks the admirable quick-detachable feature of the 1859 percussion cap alarm. It employs a turn screw to hold the wood screw in place. The rounded plate on the side provides a container for cartridges. To get a cartridge out of the container, the plate must be unscrewed.

The cartridge alarm, figure 100, is very simple and effective. Two screws hold it to a door or window frame. It shoots a .32 S & W center-fire blank. I feel its operation is so obvious it requires no explanation.

The small and cheaply made cartridge alarm shown in figure 101 has a hammer that swings through a long arc when released

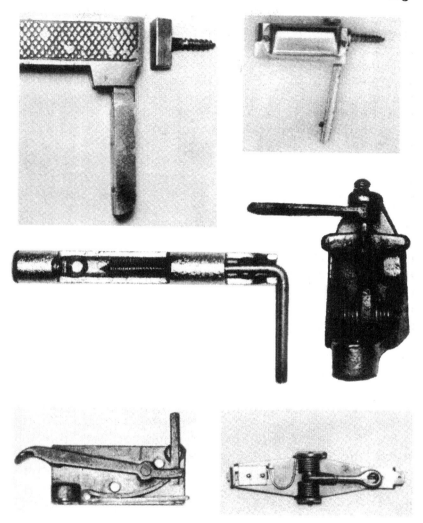

98. American Portable Alarm/ Eddie Reider collection.

99. Reiff & McDowell Alarm/ Paul J. Westergard collection.

100. Door alarm/ Governor Gordon Persons collection.

101. Unmarked alarm/ Eddie Reider collection.

102. Reichard's Alarm/ Eddie Reider collection.

103. Model Alarm/ Dr. W. R. Funderburg collection.

by movement of the protruding arm. Maybe its design was suggested by the mouse traps that pinioned their victims when the bait was touched.

The alarm in figure 102 is another of simple construction. Pressure on the protruding arm releases a long striker to fire a .22. It is marked REICHARD'S PAT. BURGLAR ALARM. It was patented December 11, 1877, patent #198,044.

The alarm shown in figure 103 again reminds us of the mouse traps. This is marked MODEL BURGLAR ALARM, CONKLIN & HAUSER, MFRS, CHICAGO. It is a product of the days when, according to its maker's statement, ammunition for it, .22 blanks, could "be purchased for ten cents per box at any hardware or gun store." (Remember when .22's came twenty-five in a box—packed loose, like tacks, not in orderly rows—priced at ten cents per box?) The Model alarm was packed in a little paper box which has printed on the side "Can be attached to any door as quickly as one can open and close the door." A direction sheet inside the box tells in detail how to attach the alarm to the door. Nine operations.

U. S. patent #286,598 was granted October 16, 1883, to Hudson Ferris of Chicago, Illinois, for the alarm shown in figure 104. The hatchet-like arm contained a cartridge, and, when the arm was slightly pushed by door or window, spring pressure threw it down so the head of the cartridge would be hit by a sharp pin in the extension of the frame. On December 28, 1886, Mr. Ferris obtained patent #335,260 for an improvement on this alarm. This improvement consisted of placing a match holder in the extreme end of the frame extension, and of serrating the head of the movable arm so a match would ignite when the alarm went off. Illustration 105 is from the patent drawing and shows the position before and after the roughened arm has struck the match head. Mr. Ferris in his specifications states the match "exposes the burglar and at once shows the location of the attempted entrance."

Twenty years before Mr. Ferris patented his "improved" match lighting alarm, Mr. A. F. Hammond, of Houston, Ohio, patented a burglar alarm with several unusual features, one of which was an arm to hold a match so it would be lighted by the burning powder when the alarm was set off. Illustration 106 is a reproduction of part of the drawing for patent #54,531 of May 8, 1866.

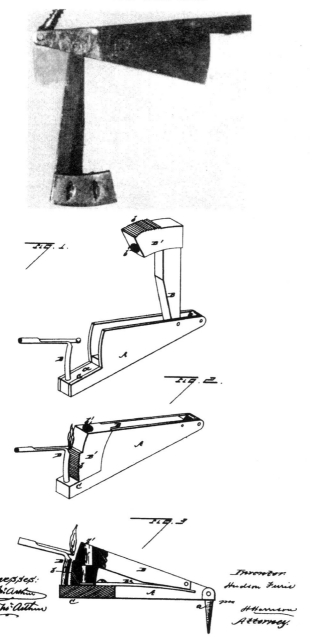

104. Ferris Alarm/ Frank R. Horner collection.

105. Ferris Alarm patent drawing.

Mr. Hammond's invention could be clamped to a mantel or any other "salient portion of the house-fitting", if the owner didn't want to fasten it to the window sill or the door frame. The drawing represents the alarm clamped over a mantel. The match, with the head at the barrel muzzle, is at the left. At the top is the end of a wire or cord, supposedly connected at the left to a door or window and shown hooked at the right to the end of a lever which when disturbed will trip a cocked hammer.

The many small caliber alarms made to be screwed to door or window frames were often frail and of low voice. The solid bronze percussion cap alarm shown in figure 107 is much different. It is placed on the floor like a door stop and it is rugged. The heavy 2¼" barrel has a bore of .40 caliber. When given a full load of black powder the alarm should be able to awaken the Seven Sleepers.

To put this alarm on duty the barrel is charged, the nipple capped, and the hammer drawn fully back until it is held by a dog catch on the end of a long sloping trigger. Then the alarm is placed on the floor close to the bottom edge of a closed door, like a door stop. Two sharp prongs on the base of the alarm at the muzzle end resist movement. If the door begins to open, the pressure will force the trigger down and release the hammer. This efficient and superior alarm was marketed in a fitted black leather case.

Illustration 108 shows a door stop alarm that fires a .22 blank instead of a percussion cap and that operates differently. When this is cocked, loaded, and placed with the small end just under the bottom edge of the door, pressure of the door on the inclined top of the wedge will force two prongs to move slightly and so release the striker.

An alarm of quite another type is shown in illustration 109. This is primarily intended as a burglar alarm that may be hung and lightly held near the top of a door by a wire inserted between the door's top rail and its frame. The alarm is in two parts that fit very loosely. The top part holds a .32 S & W blank; the bottom part has a sharp pin capable of detonating the cartridge primer. The illustration shows the alarm taken apart for loading, and with a cord running from the top part to the bent wire which will suspend the alarm several feet off the floor. Opening of the door frees the wire and lets the alarm drop. When the heavy

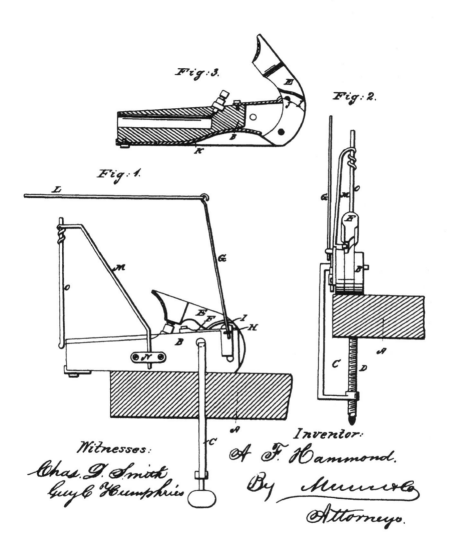

106. Hammond Alarm patent drawing.

end hits the floor the firing pin is driven against the cartridge primer. The alarm may be placed at the top of a window or in any other place where it may be lightly held, and where the alarm may have a long free drop against a hard surface.

Most alarm guns are designed to warn of unlawful entry to a room, through a door or window. Some are intended to warn of any disturbance to a locked or closed drawer, or trunk, or desk. The interesting combination of alarm gun and alarm bell shown in figure 110 could be set up to operate when a desk or trunk lid was opened. There is a striking arm running to the center of the metal plate that may be cocked against pressure of a heavy spring. When the desk or trunk lid is opened a lever moves and disengages the striker whose edge swings hard against the rim of a .22 cartridge held in the very short barrel. The lever, located across the bell from the striker, also starts prolonged ringing of the bell. The bell is the sort that when wound will ring continuously until it runs down.

An unusual Belgian alarm gun marked LE GENDARME is in figure 111. This has in back of the hammer a turntable with four arms. Three of the arms have cords tied to them. These cords are run out in different directions and secured. The fourth arm may be swung over the end of the hammer to hold it at full cock. This arm will be dislodged and the hammer tripped if an intruder runs foul of any cord and puts strain on it. Release of the hammer fires a 12 gauge center-fire shell. The barrel is held to the frame by a stout pin which when removed permits removal of the barrel for loading. The gun is fastened immovably, so no pull on the cords will move it.

If an intruder happens to be in the line of fire he may be hit by a charge from one of these alarm guns, but the alarm gun will not move around to take aim. Most trap guns, however, will do just that. At least, with the victim's unwilling co-operation they will point the barrels toward the intruder and fire when on the target.

Illustration 112 shows an English flintlock trap gun of a type well established and very unpopular a hundred and fifty years ago. Unpopular, that is, with the intended victims, poachers and grave robbers. The metal parts of such guns were all about on the same pattern, as were the two-piece wooden mounts. The wood casing afforded some protection against the weather, and

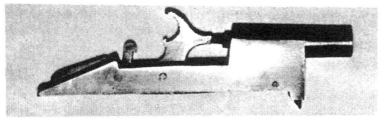

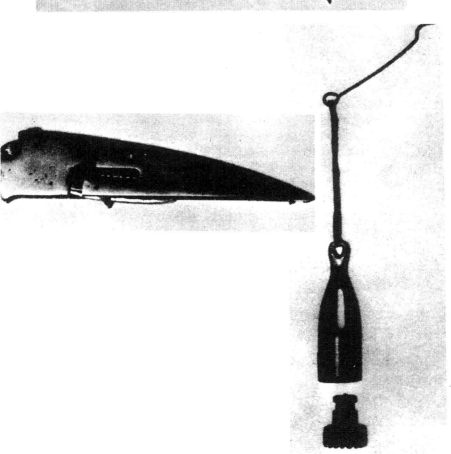

107. Doorstop alarm—5¾" overall/ Dr. W. R. Funderburg collection.

108. Doorstop alarm/ Governor Gordon Persons collection.

109. Drop alarm.

in addition there was usually a metal cover over the lock, to keep the priming powder dry. In England the setting of these trap guns was forbidden by law in 1827, according to J. N. George in *English Guns & Rifles*.

The gun was set up on a wooden base which had a hole bored in it to receive a loosely fitted pin attached to the under part of the stock. The gun was left free to rotate, and could have the muzzle elevated or depressed slightly by means of a screw fastening. The gun was fired when the cocked hammer was released by a pull on the long rod under the stock. At the end of the rod there are three rings, from each of which a wire was run and attached to some stationary object close to the ground. Such a line was called a spring, and from that came "spring gun", the usual name in England for one of these trap or set guns. The three wires spread out to encompass a rather small arc of a circle. The tightening of a line when a poacher tripped on it would swing the gun on the target and then fire it. This particular mantrap gun has a safety, which is not commonly found on these pieces. The safety is of the simplest, being just a hook that may be turned to prevent the forward motion of the rod which acts as a trigger.

A rare book, *Diary of a Resurrectionist 1811-1812*, by James Blake Bailey, in the Medical Library of King's College, Newcastle upon Tyne, attests that spring guns were set in attempts to prevent grave robbers stealing bodies to sell to anatomists. To quote Mr. Bailey,—"Besides watching, many other devices were tried to prevent the depredations of the resurrection-men; spring guns were set in many of the cemeteries but these were often rendered harmless. If the men intended going to a certain grave at night, late in the afternoon a woman, in deep mourning, would walk round the part of the cemetery in which the grave was situated, and contrive to detach the wires from the guns."

Many different designs of trap guns have been marketed. Some have sold widely. All are designed to fire at any marauder who disturbs a stretched cord, or bait. Usually only one cord or wire is used. Otherwise the various traps differ but slightly in manner of operation from the flint piece just described.

A fine early seventeenth century wheel lock trap gun, of which very few good examples exist, is shown in illustration 113. This German ambush gun was intended to guard the treasure room

110. Bell alarm/ Eddie Reider collection.

111. Gendarme alarm—7" overall/ Eddie Reider collection.

or to protect the home. A hole in the stock near the butt permitted fastening to a post or other base. The excellent lock is equipped with a set trigger. This trigger may be touched off either by a pull on a wire that runs through the stock, or by pressure on a rod that runs under the stock. This is a powerful piece, with a bore of about .75 caliber.

A French trap gun, commonly called a "chicken thief gun", is shown in figure 114. This is flintlock, all steel, marked REGNIER, and may be fastened by its clamp to any suitable support. It is not intended to have the freedom of movement of most trap guns, as it is pointed at the door or window to which the cord is attached and through which the thief is expected to try to make his entrance. Illustration 115 shows a similar but later all-metal "chicken thief gun". This uses pin-fire cartridges. Both guns have triggers that may be set to trip the hammers at the lightest touch. The set screw for the flint gun goes through the trigger guard, while that for the pin-fire goes through the bar under the barrel. An unusual feature of the pin-fire is that the stretched cord goes around a little wheel under the muzzle and up to the long bar, so the gun is discharged by the bar's being pulled down rather than out. It is clear that both of these guns could be used as conventional pocket pistols.

An all-brass gun that may be called a mantrap cannon is shown in figure 116. This uses a pin-fire cartridge of about .70 caliber, and is secured by a 2½" wood screw, pointing at you in the illustration. The breech piece turns on a pivot for loading. The striker is attached directly to the mainspring. The striker may be held cocked by the short end of a pivoted arm until that arm is disturbed by strain on a cord attached to the long end of the arm. The gun is shown cocked, with the breech open.

The bronze percussion cap two-barrel trap gun in illustration 117 is shown as seen from above when the horseshoe frame is set on a horizontal base. The post in the center is hollow. Supposedly, it fits over a pin in the base so the gun may rotate. A pull on a cord attached to a rod running midway between the barrels will swing the barrels in line with the target and then release the cocked hammers. The illustration shows one hammer cocked, with the nipple not yet capped, but it is likely that both hammers would usually be cocked and both barrels fired together. This gun bears a partly obliterated name and date. I found no

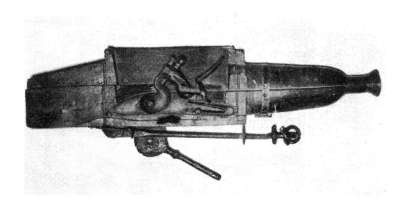

112. Spring gun 19½″ overall/ Robert Abels collection.

113. Trap gun/ Major Leo E. Huff collection.

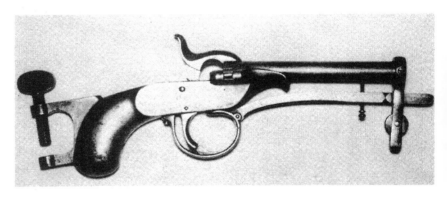

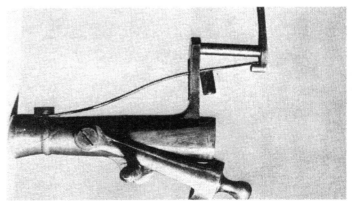

114. "Chicken Thief" gun—9" overall/ Gov. Gordon Persons collection.

115. "Chicken Thief" gun/ Eddie Reider collection.

116. Trap gun/ Hampton P. Howell, Jr. collection.

record of a patent. Of course, I could have missed it.

It is not unusual to find names and dates, and sometimes "Patent applied for" or even "Patented" on odd firearms for which the inventor never succeeded in obtaining a patent. The remaining illustrations and descriptions in this chapter are of more-or-less successful trap guns for which United States patents were granted.

Each of the four different percussion cap trap pistols on plate 118 is marked F. REUTHE'S PATENT. The one at the bottom, with the spring compressed, is in before-firing position. The three others, with their barbs thrown wide, are in after-firing position. Each trap gun has two barrels firing together, one at either side of a tube into which the two-pronged barbed spring is forced back when the trap is set. These trap guns, made of iron, have barrels from 3½" to 5" in length, with calibers from .28 to .50.

Large quantities of trap pistols were made in Hartford, Connecticut, under Mr. Reuthe's patent #17,297, of May 12, 1857. Some were marked with the place of manufacture and/or the patent date in addition to the maker's name.

Most of these harrowing devices, referred to in the patent papers as "Jaw Traps", or "Traps for Capturing and Destroying Wild Animals", were constructed with nipples at right angles to the barrels and were cocked by pulling down a heavy mainspring located under the barrels. The one at the top of the illustration has nipples in line with the barrels and is cocked by pulling back a heavy striker. The second from the top has a screwed-in pistol grip which may be replaced with the regulation ringed-end rod designed to fasten the piece to a tree or stake.

In operation, bait was fastened to "the peculiar sliding and expanding springs". These springs were pressed back into the tube between the barrels where they would engage the hammer when the latter was cocked. With the trap baited, the barrels loaded, the nipples capped, and the hammers cocked, "The victim seizes the bait and pulling it to devour it, the springs . . . slide forward . . . the hammers fall forcibly, . . . discharging the balls down the throat, at the same instant the springs expand in the animal's mouth the barbs and fangs hold him fast".

Mr. George Smith obtained patent #32,539 on June 11, 1861, for an invention he described as a "Combined Burglar-Alarm and Animal-Trap". The example shown in illustration 119 is all iron

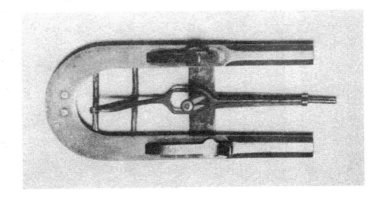

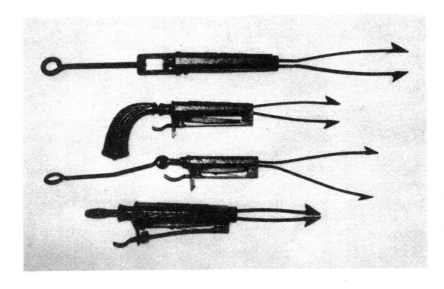

117. "Horse shoe" gun/ Eddie Reider collection.

118. Group Reuthe trap guns/ Eddie Reider collection.

and has three muzzle-loading .34 caliber barrels bored side by side and parallel. Vents lead from the single nipple to all three barrels, so detonation of a cap fires the three charges in unison. Mr. Smith's patent drawing shows a single barrel gun, but Mr. Smith states, "a plurality of barrels may be used".

With the wood screw properly secured the barrels have a traverse of about 120°. As Mr. Smith points out, bait may be attached to the wire loop at the muzzle, if the device is used as an animal trap, or, if it is used as a burglar alarm, cords may be run from the loop to one or more doors or windows.

On June 28, 1859, John O. Couch and Henry S. North obtained patent #24,573 for an invention they described as a "Game-Shooter". Two of these percussion cap trap guns are shown in figures 120 and 121.

This product of Connecticut is said to have found favor in Australia, for trapping kangaroos. It is much like the Reuthe, illustration 118, in operation, except that it does not use the barbed springs. Bait was attached close in front of the muzzle by a short cord. The gun was suspended by a cord or chain running from a branch of a tree to the eye on the backstrap. The gun was pointed and fired when the unfortunate animal took the bait. The cylinder has six barrels, bored either parallel or spreading slightly apart at the muzzle. There is one nipple only. Fire from an exploded cap passes through the nipple and around an annular channel so all six barrels are discharged practically simultaneously. Either of the guns illustrated may be fired by pulling the trigger or by pulling the rod whose end protrudes at the muzzle. The small and scarce one has a conventional hammer. The larger one—the one much more frequently found—has a large round sliding striker.

These North and Couch guns could of course be used as hand guns either for self-defense or murder, but any one who reads inventors' patent specifications will realize all inventors are convinced that hand guns will serve no purpose but self-defense.

Mr. George Pratt obtained patent #290,605 on December 18, 1883, for an invention he described as an "efficient fire-arm for protecting orchards and vineyards from the depredations of animals and thieves". This all-metal percussion cap device, illustration 122, has two 4" barrels of about .38 caliber which are fastened together so they converge slightly at the muzzle. The

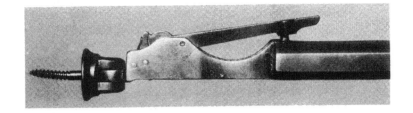

119. George Smith Trap gun/ Dr. W. R. Funderburg collection.

120. North & Couch Trap gun.

121. North & Couch Trap gun/ William M. Locke collection.

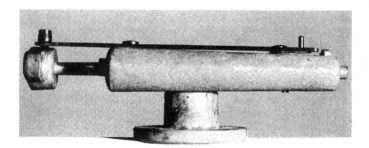

PRATT'S

BURGLAR ALARM AND ANIMAL TRAP.

DIRECTIONS FOR SETTING THE ALARM.

Screw the socket (A) to a small piece of board or to a post. Then load one or both barrels with blank charge, and place the Alarm where you wish it to stand. Then take a fine thread or wire, pass it through hole (B), and fasten the end in hole (C). Then carry the other end to any distance you wish it to cover. Stretch comparatively taut, and secure to some stationary object. Then take the barrels out of socket (A), and place the hammer-rod (D) against something, and push the hammer back till the trigger engages with the roll on hammer. Then place the barrels back in socket (A), and put on the caps.

Use Union Metalic Cartridge Cos.'s Caps No. 11.

MIDDLETOWN, CONN.

122. Pratt Trap gun/ Frank R. Horner collection.

123. Pratt Instruction sheet/ Courtesy John Hintlian.

barrel assembly has an underneath stud to be slipped into a bearing on a platform base so the gun may rotate full circle.

It was once suggested to me that cords were fastened to these trap guns in such a way that disturbance of a cord would move the barrels out of line with the intruder. Lest any one accept such a statement as applying to this gun, I quote from Mr. Pratt's specification: "If the barrels should not be in line with the animal when it comes in contact with the cord, it will be obvious that slight pressure on the cord will rotate the barrels and bring them substantially into line with the intruder, thus killing or injuring the same when the barrels are discharged."

It is difficult to reconcile that quoted sentence, which surely implies the barrels were loaded with ball, with the instructions on the direction sheet which call for loading with a blank charge. A reproduction of an original direction sheet is shown in illustration 123.

The main difference between the two trap guns shown in figures 124 and 125 is that the one made fast with the wood screw is .22 caliber, while the one with the long heavy pin is 10 gauge. The .22, which has a brass barrel and a brass frame, is marked TAYLOR FUR GETTER, F. C. TAYLOR FUR CO., ST. LOUIS, MO. and PAT'D JUNE 2, 1914. The 10 gauge which has a steel barrel and a bronze frame, is unmarked. Both guns conform to the specifications of the patent granted C. D. Lovelace on June 2, 1914, patent #1,098,742.

The Lovelace trap gun, or Fur Getter as it was usually called, was cocked by pulling a striker straight back, and fired by pulling the bait rod forward. This rod could be fitted in different positions to change barrel elevation. The barrel was removed for loading by turning the bent handle of a retaining pin, and this pin could be used for turning the heavy wood screw. Mr. Lovelace had some ingenious ideas and he had no doubt as to the efficacy of his invention. Speaking of an animal taking the bait, he says, ". . . it receives the missile discharged from the gun and is killed thereby".

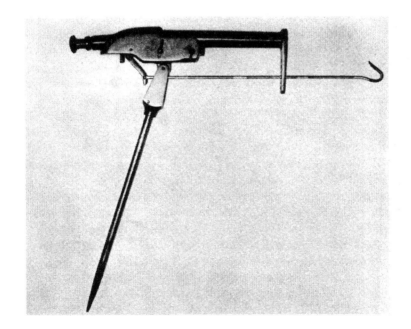

124. Trap gun/ Eddie Reider collection.

125. Trap gun/ Governor Gordon Persons collection.

Chapter 7

KNIFE PISTOLS AND CANE GUNS

KNIFE PISTOLS and cane guns belong to our fathers' and grand-fathers' days. Some, made before the little .22 rim-fire cartridge was invented, used percussion cap ignition, but it was only following the widespread production of the .22 short that these disguised weapons of surprise enjoyed a mild popularity.

It seems fitting to bracket the knife pistols and cane guns in one chapter, apart from other disguised and hidden guns, and from other combination weapons. The grandfather who walked abroad carrying a cane gun may well have had a knife pistol in his pocket.

Probably the most widely sold and best known knife pistol is the Unwin & Rodgers. This was first made as a muzzle-loader using percussion caps; later as a breechloader using rim-fire cartridges. Illustration 126 shows a cartridge model at the top and a percussion cap model below. Each has horn handles and two folding blades. Each has a small trap with a hinged cover in the grip. The hammers and folding triggers are similar in construction on the two models. Both pieces have Birmingham proof marks. An interesting feature of the percussion cap model is the inclusion of two accessories shown in the photograph. One is a bullet mold and one is a ramrod. Both accessories have spring ends so they will be held in place by friction when pushed in the slots cut in the knife handles.

An Unwin & Rodgers knife pistol of unusual construction is shown in figure 127. As in the upper pistol shown in figure 126

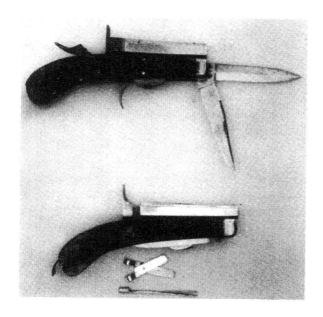

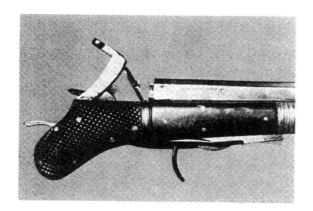

126. Two Unwin & Rodgers knife pistols.
Upper, Oscar J. Rees collection—lower, Paul J. Westergard collection.

127. Unwin & Rodgers knife pistol/ Eddie Reider collection.

there is an extractor which when pulled back draws the fired case from the chamber. However, in this gun it is necessary, after the hammer is cocked, to raise a hinged piece like a false breech before the extractor may be drawn back. The gun is shown with this piece raised and the extractor pulled back.

The knife pistols just described are marked UNWIN & RODGERS, SHEFFIELD. Other knife pistols on the same pattern are found marked JAMES RODGERS, SHEFFIELD.

One of the rare two-barrel Rodgers knife pistols is illustrated in figure 128. This is by James Rodgers and has "Self Protector" marked on the two large blades which are set in the middle with a small blade on the right and another on the left. These rather heavy and awkward pieces were not formed by joining two ordinary knife pistols, but were specially manufactured.

Another type knife pistol that was widely sold in this country is the little all metal penknife which does not at a glance reveal itself as being also a firearm. Figure 129 shows the knife with the firing lever visible on the side and with the very short cartridge chamber and barrel tilted for loading. The hammer normally lies flat against the side of the knife; it is flipped up to cock, and pressed down with a quick squeeze to fire. The space between the two sides of the knife is divided lengthwise into two narrow compartments. One contains two knife blades; the other contains the coiled mainspring, the trigger, the firing pin and finally the .22 cartridge in its very short barrel. The piece illustrated is unmarked but it conforms fully with the specifications for the "Pocket Firearm" patented February 29, 1916, by Leo Louis Rogers, patent #1,173,464.

The penknife pistol illustrated in figure 130 is much like the Leo Louis Rogers knife pistol just described except it has a firing lever which folds into the knife casing, and it is marked "Defender".

Another all metal knife pistol, illustration #131, is a little larger, but of the same general construction, and apparently of the same make as the "Defender". This larger jacknife size was the "Huntsman", according to the advertisement in the March, 1922 issue of *Popular Science Monthly*. The advertisement which states the gun has a thousand uses and which illustrates one use, is reproduced in figure 132. The "Defender" was offered in the 1923 catalogue of N. Shure Co., Chicago, at $3.25.

The "Defender" and the "Huntsman" are at the end of the

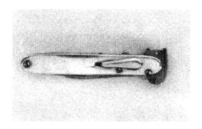

128. James Rodgers knife pistol.

129. Knife pistol/ Oscar J. Rees collection.

130. Knife pistol/ Caleb J. Westergard collection.

131. Knife pistol/ Arnott J. Millett collection.

132. Reproduction of advertisement/ Courtesy Paul J. Westergard.

knife-pistol era, at least in this country. The Peavey knife pistols may have marked the beginning of the era. Mr. A. J. Peavey obtained patent #49784 on Sept. 5, 1865, for a percussion cap "Knife and Pistol", and also patent #53473 on March 27, 1866, for a "Combined Pistol & Knife" using a rim-fire cartridge. A cartridge model is shown in illustration #133 and a reproduction of the patent drawing for the percussion cap model in illustration 134. The long hammer, when down and resting in the frame of the knife, looks like a second knife blade. The trigger is concealed in the knife casing when the hammer is down. In the operation of either model the hammer is pulled up against heavy spring pressure until the inner end of an arm of the trigger engages a notch and causes the hammer to be propped up in the cocked position. Pressure on the trigger will disengage the hammer and let it crash down.

It is interesting to notice that the Peavey knife pistol will also serve as an alarm. As Mr. Peavey wrote in his patent specification, "The trigger may be pulled by hand, or, if the pistol is to be used as an alarm, a cord may be secured to the end of the trigger and drawn through a channel, k, in the butt end of the handle. By securing the knife in some appropriate place in a room and tying the end of the cord to the doorlatch or to a window the trigger will be pulled in case somebody attempts to open the door or to raise the window and the charge of the barrel is exploded. If desired, the knife-blade may be stuck into the casing of the door, so that the door, on being opened, strikes the trigger and explodes the charge."

Figure 135 is of a two-bladed pocketknife that very cleverly conceals a .22 cartridge pistol. The folding hammer is visible only when pulled down for cocking, as shown in the illustration. The trigger is the center screw head in the bone handle. Pressing this button trigger releases the hammer.

An early percussion cap knife pistol which very thoroughly disguises the fact it is a firearm is shown in figure 136. This horn-handled piece is normally carried with the single knife blade closed and lying alongside the long hammer in the frame. The appearance is then of an ordinary knife with two blades, the gun barrel and the nipple for the cap being both hidden in the frame. When the hammer is cocked, as shown in the illustration, it may be released by a slight forward pressure, when it will

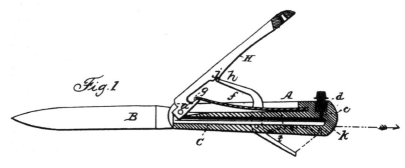

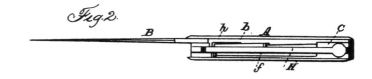

Inventor:

a L Peavey

By Munn Co

atty

133. Peavey knife pistol/ Robert Abels collection.
134. Peavey patent drawing.

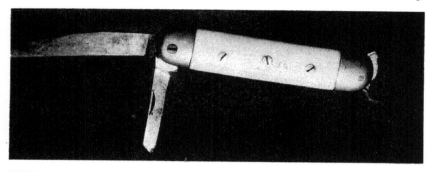

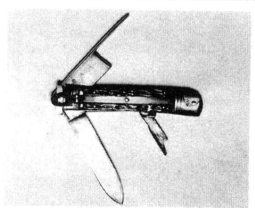

135. Knife pistol/ Frank R. Horner collection.

136. Knife pistol/ Frank R. Horner collection.

137. Knife pistol/ Harold G. Young collection.

be driven hard against the cap.

A German knife pistol marked BAZAR, and SPRINGER and SOLIN-GEN is shown in figure 137. The barrel is shown raised to permit loading a cartridge. The hammer is the trigger-like projection under the frame. The trigger is a small button. At one end of the stag horn handle is a swinging ring which permits the knife blade to be locked open or closed. Lying under this ring is shown an extractor, marked "C-12", for 12-gauge shells. On the opposite side, marked "C-16", is an extractor for 16-gauge shells. Such extractors are still frequently supplied on German pocket knives. They are used to pry from shotgun barrels partially ejected shells that have become misshapen and stuck as the result of repeated use.

This little extracting device is perhaps shown more clearly in figure 138, which illustrates another model of a BAZAR pistol. Here the button trigger is clearly visible, and the striker is seen to be a plunger with a knob on the end. A cartridge is shown partially inserted in the chamber of the short barrel.

A scarcer type of German pocketknife pistol is pictured in figure 139. This uses pin-fire ignition and is fitted with three blades. To fire the gun—simply raise the hammer, insert a cartridge and pull the trigger.

In figure 140 is another pin-fire knife pistol which could be made to serve as an alarm pistol by screwing the gimlet end of the trigger so it could be moved back by pressure of an opening door. This is European, marked MARTI on the blade. The piece is shown with the barrel raised for loading. Pressure on the ornamental panel set in the bone handle moves a catch which locks the barrel when the latter is down.

Two special purpose knife pistols which have percussion cap ignition are represented in figures 141 and 142. Number 141 is a horseman's knife. Hinged at one end of the knife is a hook for cleaning horse's hooves. This hoof hook will also serve as a grip for the pistol. The pointed trigger is threaded like a wood-screw. One way to convert the piece to an alarm gun would be to screw the trigger into wood and let movement of the knife fire the gun. Number 142 is a sailor's knife pistol. This all-metal product has a marlinspike at one end and is shown with the hammer down and the trigger folded. It is also more elaborate than most knife pistols, with raised decorations on the sides

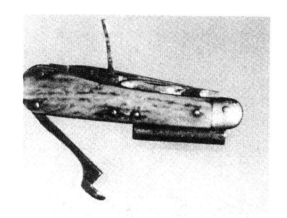

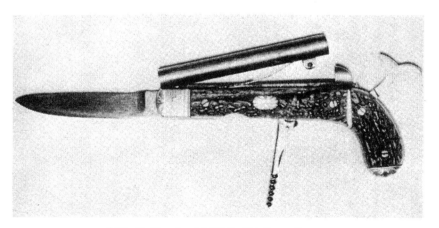

138. Knife pistol/ Eddie Réider collection.

139. Knife pistol/ Anthony A. Fidd collection.

140. Knife pistol/ Eddie Reider collection.

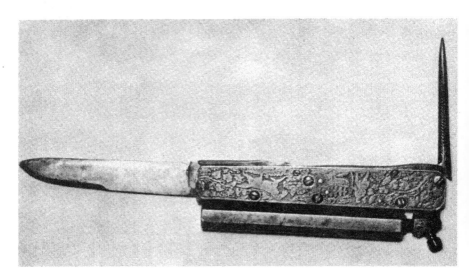

141. Horseman's knife pistol/ Anthony A. Fidd collection.

142. Sailor's knife pistol/ Eddie Reider collection.

showing hunters and animals. The octagon barrel has fine poly-groove rifling. On both these percussion cap pieces the barrels are full length and also in full view, quite unlike the short and hidden barrels of the later cartridge inventions.

Some knife pistols have been produced with blade cases formed like pistol grips. A fine specimen is shown in illustration #143. This has two side-by-side finely figured Damascus barrels of about .36 caliber with two hammers and two triggers for percussion cap ignition. There is a finely decorated brass frame into which fold the two triggers and the heavy dagger blade.

A knife pistol with conventional pistol grips fitted to the knife casing is shown in figure #144. Here the knife plays a minor role but fully retains its identity. The piece is a combination of a bolt-action firearm and a pocket knife, not merely a firearm with a blade attached. This is the LITTLE PAL. It is marked L. E. POLHEMUS MFG CO. MIAMI ARIZONA and LITTLE PAL MODEL 23—.22 SHORTS ONLY. There is nothing unusual about the bolt action except the fact it is being used in a knife pistol instead of in a rifle.

It may be well to add a word about the cartridges used in LITTLE PAL. The .22 shorts when first made about a hundred years ago, would drive a bullet an inch or more into wood. The knife pistols that used those cartridges were rightly regarded as dangerous weapons. In the most favoring conditions a bullet from a knife pistol could put a man beyond mortal aid in one tick of time. The cartridges are no less powerful now and man's body tissues are no more resistant now.

Between the knife pistols and the cane guns we admit in this chapter a combination of clasp knife and revolver, illustration #145. The revolver is of Belgian make, 6-shot, 5mm in caliber, double-action, superposed on the frame of a knife having a long curved blade. Pleasing in color are the sides of the knife, made of horn and all one with the grips of the revolver.

The pistols combined with pocketknives do not go as far back as cane guns. Though knife pistols do not antedate the invention of the percussion cap, walking sticks combined with flint pistols are to be found.

In the lexicon of the American collector any walking stick combined with a firearm is a cane gun whether or not cane is used in the construction. Some cane guns are all-metal.

In 1814 a British patent #3837 was granted Henry William

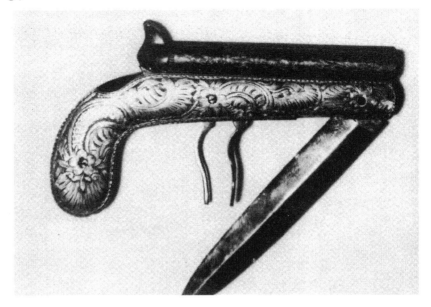

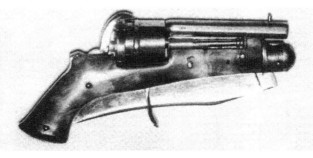

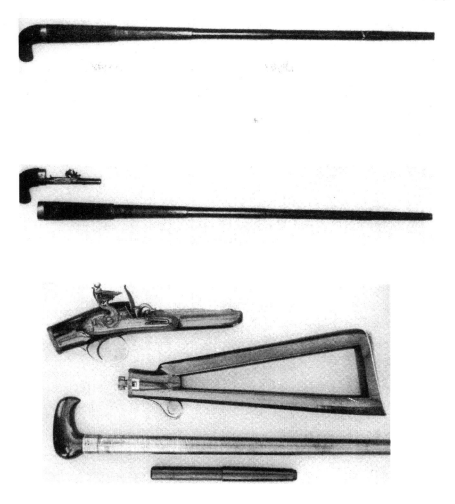

146. and 147. Cane gun/ Dr. W. R. Funderburg collection.
148. Walking stick gun/ W. Keith Neal collection.

(Opposite page)

143. Knife pistol/ Governor Gordon Persons collection.
144. Little Pal/ Eddie Reider collection.
145. Knife revolver/ Frank R. Horner collection.

Vander Kleft for a "Method of Construction" of a "Walking Staff" that was passing strange. This eccentricity was in nine parts to contain, among other things, a folding trigger flintlock pistol, kept in the cane at half cock and with the pan fastened down. The cap or head of the staff is an inkstand; the ferrule is a two-compartment container for gunpowder and pistol balls. Space is provided between the pistol and the ferrule for pen, pencil, paper, drawing utensils, knife, turnscrew for the pistol, and a telescope. Walking sticks combining flintlock pistols and tele-scopes were made by Mr. Kleft. There may exist a cane such as his patent described.

Illustrations 146 and 147 give two views of an English cane that conceals a flint pistol. The pistol may be quickly pulled out of the solid wood staff when a spring is pressed. In the cane the loaded and primed pistol is held at half cock by a sliding safety. A concealed folding trigger comes out when the pistol is with-drawn and the hammer cocked. The steel frame of the gun is marked PRICE INVENTOR and 221 STRAND, LONDON. The screw-barrel has Birmingham proof marks.

In illustration 148 a special purpose flint cane gun is shown. This is a poacher's gun. The two parts of the stock are carried concealed but the barrel of the gun is carried openly as a cane, being fitted at the breech with a special handle and at the muzzle with a tampion resembling a cane tip. This is a piece of very fine workmanship, made by T. Squires, London. The furniture is silver which bears the hallmarked assayer's date of 1812. Be-cause of the high quality of this shotgun, one may well doubt it was actually built for poaching use.

Probably the Day's Patent Cane was the most popular and widely sold of percussion cap canes. It was also a very early one, being patented by John Day, Barnstaple, Devon, England in 1823, British patent #4861.

The cane gun at the top of each of the illustrations 149 and 150 is a Day's Patent. In 150 the cocked gun is shown with the ramrod and long tampion out of the barrel. In the other illus-tration the ramrod is hidden in the barrel and the tampion is inserted in the muzzle. This cane has on the handle a silver plate, presentation inscribed and dated 1859. After thirty-six years the model apparently was still popular.

Two views of an unmarked but probably French pepperbox

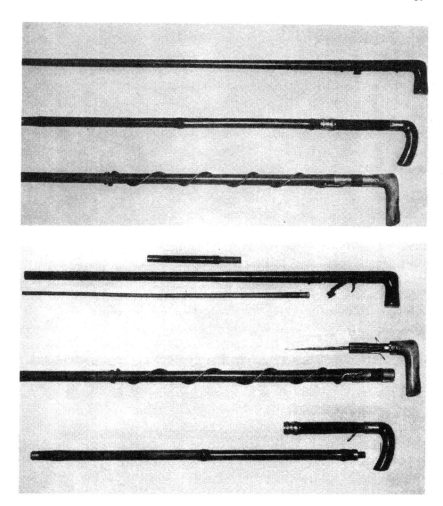

149. and 150. Group of cane guns.
        Day's Patent Cane is from John L. Barry, Jr. collection.

cane are also shown in illustrations 149 and 150. The pepperbox is six-shot and double-action with a folding trigger. The cartridge used is a very small caliber rim-fire. There is a slender and very weak blade that projects from the center of the cylinder. The gun may be withdrawn from the cane when a release button in the grip is pressed. This pepperbox, like the flint pistol in illustration 146, must be withdrawn from the cane to be put in action, the shaft of the cane being a solid piece of wood. Around this shaft is entwined a realistic brass serpent. In the Day's Patent Cane the shaft of the cane, of iron, is itself the barrel. The third cane shown in this group of three has an iron barrel encased in cane or bamboo. This cane unscrews to load a .32 cartridge, is cocked by pulling back the handle, and fired by pressing a folding trigger. It has no marks and its provenience is unknown. The silver bands on it and also the bands on the pepperbox cane effectively conceal the presence of a firearm in either piece.

The Remingtons are the best known American cane guns. Figure 151 reproduces an advertisement which appeared in the *George W. Hawes' Ohio State Gazetteer and Business Directory for 1859 and 1860.* This percussion cap model was patented Feb. 9, 1858, by J. F. Thomas, of Ilion, New York, U.S. patent #19328. Mr. Thomas' claims had to do with the ingenious method of combining the barrel and the case surrounding the action ". . . so as to make the implement safe, cheap, and effective . . ." To cap the nipple the handle, including the casing around the action, was drawn back until a flat spring-catch jumped up and prevented forward motion of the casing. The gun was now cocked and could be fired after capping the nipple, by pressing a small button trigger which released the long striker. The tip of the catch, or stop, which held back the casing served also as a rear sight. Pressing down on the sight, and forward on the handle, let down the hammer without discharging the gun.

Instead of a tight solid ferrule made of wood or metal, to close the end of the barrel, Mr. Thomas provided an open screw-in ferrule with a small piece of cork in its lower end. The bit of cork was held by friction only, and would be carried out by the ball in the event of accidental discharge. Usually in other cane guns a wooden tampion served as a ferrule. Such a plug, tightly fitted and accidently left in when the gun was discharged, might cause a burst barrel. Loosely fitted, it might drop out and be lost.

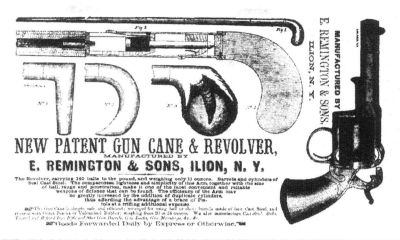

NEW PATENT GUN CANE & REVOLVER,

MANUFACTURED BY
E. REMINGTON & SONS, ILION, N. Y.

This Revolver, carrying 140 balls to the pound, and weighing only 11 ounces. Barrels and cylinders of best Cast Steel. The compactness, lightness and simplicity of this Arm, together with the size of ball, range and penetration, make it one of the most convenient and reliable weapons of defence that can be found. The efficiency of the Arm may be greatly increased by the addition of duplicate cylinders, thus affording the advantage of a brace of Pistols at a trifling additional expense.

☞ The Gun Cane is simple, safe and efficient; arranged for using ball or shot; barrels made of best Cast Steel, and covered with Gutta Percha or Vulcanized Rubber; weighing from 20 to 24 ounces. We also manufacture *Cast Steel, Sile, Twist and Round Iron Rifle and Shot Gun Barrels, Gun Locks, Gun Mountings, &c. &c.*

☞ Goods Forwarded Daily by Express or Otherwise.☜

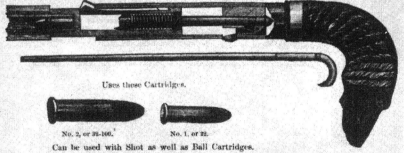

The Remington Rifle Cane.

JUST THE THING FOR TAXIDERMISTS.

No. 1 Cane weighs 16 oz. No. 2, 24 oz.

Protection against Dogs and Highwaymen.

Uses these Cartridges.

No. 2, or 32-100.   No. 1, or 22.

Can be used with Shot as well as Ball Cartridges.

PRICE LIST.

Rifle Canes	$10·00 each.
" Ivory Head	15 00 "
Cartridges, No. 1	6 00 per M
" " 2. Short	12 00 "
Shot Cartridges, No. 1	12 00 "
" " 2	17 00 "

151. From the New York Historical Society/ Courtesy John E. Parsons.

152. From Bella C. Landauer Collection at the N. Y. Historical Society.

An 1878 Remington catalogue advertisement of a Remington Rifle Cane is shown in figure 152. It will be seen that the mechanism for this cartridge cane is quite like that for the percussion cap cane.

Incidentally, the revolver pictured with that first model cane is the earliest model Beal's patent.

Illustration 153 shows a percussion cap model Remington Rifle Cane. This has a claw-and-ball handle and a 27" rifled barrel covered with gutta percha.

In figure 154 is a scarce snake handler's cane which might be looked at for some time by anyone unfamiliar with its properties without his knowing it concealed a powerful and efficient gun. Figure 155 is another view of this all-metal cane with a snake handler's hook, or pick-up, for a handle. If you have watched a snake handler pick up a rattler from a Florida snake pit, you have probably seen him use a staff with such a hook on the end. This gun is a small bore percussion cap shotgun which, as the second illustration shows, must have the barrel completely unscrewed for capping. To cock the gun a short section near the hook is pulled back with a turning motion until the concealed trigger is fully open. When the handle is pushed back the gun is ready to fire, assuming of course that the barrel has been loaded, capped and screwed into position, with the barrel plug removed. The barrel plug is the usual wooden tampion with brass covered tip. The trigger will fold back and blend so well with the all-steel shaft that it is invisible except on careful examination.

A group of canes is pictured in illustration 156. The two canes at the top are alike. They are beautifully made with silvered handles. One of these has the tampion pulled out of the barrel muzzle, and the handle unscrewed so a cartridge may be loaded. Pulling back the striker knob and then pressing the button trigger fires the cartridge. In this instance the tampion is metal and has spring ends to hold it in the barrel.

Just below the pair of canes is another dapper cane that very efficiently masks a concealed gun. Its construction is unusual and a little complicated. A cartridge may be chambered when the handle is drawn back slightly. Cocking is accomplished by pressing the handle firmly against the barrel section and locking it by a slight turn. The trigger is the very small horn button that protrudes only slightly underneath the horn handle. There is an

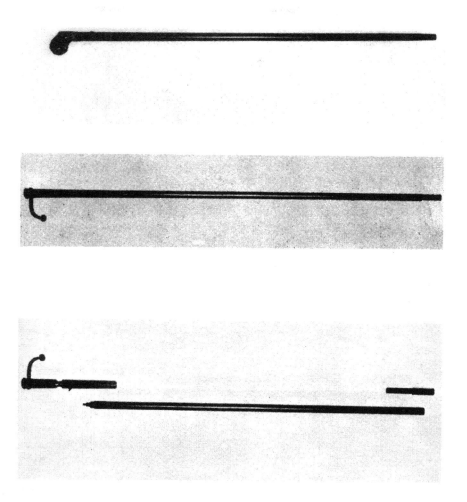

153. Remington Cane/ Frank R. Horner collection.

154. and 155. Snake handler's cane/ Eddie Reider collection.

extractor that draws out any cartridge or fired shell when the handle is pulled back.

The remaining cane in this group is a stout walking stick that becomes a gun only after singular manipulation. To transform the cane to a shoulder arm the long handle is turned to permit loading a cartridge and then moved to the position shown in the photograph. After that the handle is pulled to cock the striker, and then pushed right back to uncover a trigger. The grip is wood. The rest of the cane is metal covered with leather.

One of the cane guns much prized by collectors is the unusual Lang percussion cane, shown in two views. Illustration 157 shows the piece as a cane; illustration 158 shows it as a shoulder gun. The change is made by pulling back the handle and turning it down. The striker is cocked with the accessory shown angling up from the firing assembly. This accessory contains a capper, and after being used as illustrated to cock the hammer and incidentally open the folding trigger, it is turned end for end and used to place a cap on the nipple. This particular cane comes in an elaborate case fully equipped with accessories. To be placed in the case the cane is unscrewed so the barrel and the stock will lie in separate fitted compartments. There is a special compartment for the combination tool used for cocking and capping and another for the striker which when in the gun is at all times unattached to any other part. In addition to these two essential parts of the gun, accessories fitted in the case include—flask, mold, nipple wrench and vent prick, oil can, box of caps, extra cane tip, and an unusual jointed ramrod with screw-on worm, rammer and scouring tips. Lang was an early nineteenth century London maker of fine firearms which often had features infrequently found in firearms of other makes.

A poacher's cane gun that is in process of either being taken down or put together is shown in illustration 159. This is a French percussion cap gun.

The reader is asked to use a little imagination. If the gun as pictured is being taken down, the lock assembly is to be pushed back in the hollowed stock and the two parts of the stock closed. The folded buttstock with the hidden firing mechanism may be concealed in a greatcoat pocket or under the clothing. The barrel with the tampion in becomes a walking staff. If the gun is being assembled for shooting, the lock assembly is to be pulled fully

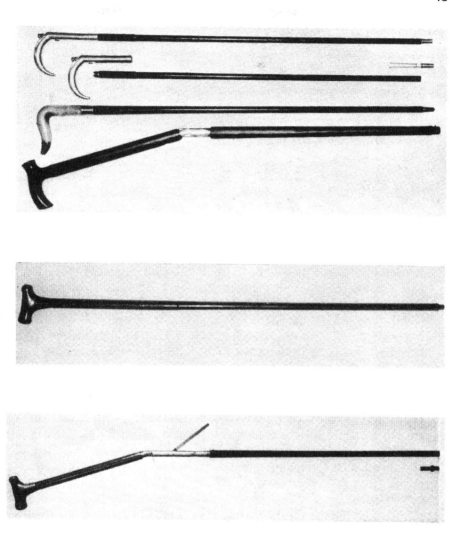

156. Group of cane guns/ Eddie Reider collection.

157. and 158. Lang Cane Gun/ Robert Abels collection.

out and screwed into the barrel. When the two parts of the hinged stock are now closed the hunter has a full length gun with shoulder stock, quite normal in appearance except it lacks a forestock.

A cane gun rarely found is pictured in illustration 160. This is a repeater, carrying in the staff a magazine loaded with .22 cartridges, and was patented by Marcelin Daigle, Houma, Louisiana, on April 10, 1877, patent #189,305. It has a composition grip and a metal body painted brown and simulating bamboo. The magazine, a long tube lying alongside the barrel, may be filled by pressing cartridges in from the breech when the handle is drawn back. With the magazine filled the operation is simple. The button on the side is pressed and the handle drawn slightly back. When the handle is pressed forward the gun fires. This reciprocating action may of course be quickly repeated. This drawing back will eject an empty shell from the barrel, place a live shell in the carrier and move it in line with the barrel chamber. Pushing forward the handle will chamber the cartridge and then release the firing pin.

All guns which use air or spring pressure to propel a charge are deliberately omitted from this volume. In illustration 161 two blow guns are shown, but they use powder for the bullet propellant. These two canes are similar in operation but slightly different in construction. Each loads a center-fire 7 mm cartridge and each uses a mouth-blown dart to detonate the primer. Each cane consists of two hollow tubes, metal covered with wood. One tube is a barrel for the bullet, the other a barrel for the floating dart. In one cane the two sections must be unscrewed for loading; in the other the two sections need be drawn only partly apart, until a cartridge may be dropped in a trough.

When the top of the silver knob of either of these canes is unscrewed the gun may be fired by blowing with some force directly against the head of the dart. That the pointed dart is free to move in the tube and is subject to the force of gravity should be kept in mind both before and when aiming.

On each cane about an inch back of the cartridge head a small hole is bored, so that a nail or rod thrust through will serve as a safety by stopping the dart. On one cane there is provided a soft rubber ring, fitted into the knob or cap and designed to prevent injury to the mouth by recoil of the gun. These canes have neither hammers nor triggers. When completely assembled

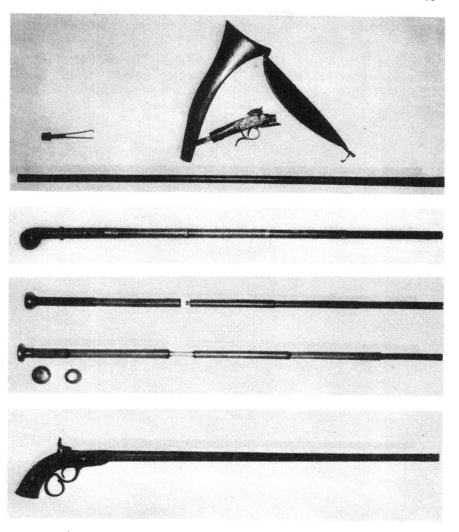

159. Poacher's cane gun/ Robert Abels collection.

160. Daigle Cane Gun/ Dr. W. R. Funderburg collection.

161. Two cane guns/ Martin B. Retting collection.

162. Perry Cane Gun.

ᴀ tampions in the muzzles they give no indication whatever
ᴇy are firearms.

I am influenced to include the gun shown in figure 162, by the
fact that collectors often call this model the "Perry Cane Gun".
This is marked PERRY PATENT ARMS CO., NEWARK, N. J. and is no
different from other Perry pistols except it has a 26¾" barrel.
It is of the type made without a capper in the butt.

Chapter 8

OTHER DISGUISED GUNS

INVENTORS have overlooked few objects that could be used to conceal a firearm. Further, these inventors have realized that the more innocent and unexpected the cover for the gun the better the chance for surprise attack.

The combining, and often concealing, of a gun or pistol with an edged weapon was not unnatural—but a man is wary of a sword and heedful of a displayed jacknife. Even a stout cane may give pause, for down through the ages clubs have dispatched more humans and animals than any other weapon.

A light riding whip causes less alarm than a cane—and a smoker's pipe none at all. Both have been made to hide pistols. Examples are now shown.

In illustrations 163 and 164 two views are shown of an English percussion cap whip pistol, unmarked except for Birmingham proofs. The lash is pulled away from the handle when the piece is to be fired or loaded. The barrel may be unscrewed, as shown, for the purpose of capping the nipple. The striker is cocked by pulling the bone knob straight back; it is released by pressing a small button trigger. All parts are covered with leather, except the bone knob.

Another combination of whip and muzzle-loading percussion cap pistol is highly original in construction and manner of operating. When fully disguised as a whip, as in illustration 165, there is a knob screwed into the barrel muzzle, and this knob in turn has a rammer screwed into it. Another knob, the one with a ring

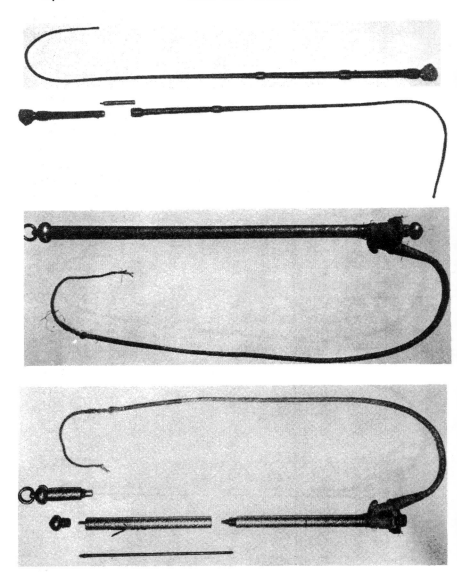

163. and 164. Whip pistol/ Dr. W. R. Funderburg collection.

165. and 166. Whip pistol/ Harold G. Young collection.

in it, is at the end of a small section of the handle which is screwed over the striker. When the gun is to be put in use both these knobs are turned off, as in illustration 166. The knob from the muzzle end has the rammer unscrewed from it. That knob may then be screwed on the protruding end of the striker, replacing the short section that has the ring at the tip. When screwed on and pulled back, it cocks the gun. The cocked firing pin is released by pressure on a trigger that lies flush with the grip until a sliding safety is pushed forward. Illustration 166 shows the knob removed from the muzzle ready to be screwed on the firing pin, and the barrel unscrewed ready for capping. The braided lash is tied to the metal gun with very intricate fastening. The gold and silver Oriental decoration of the metal is in a pleasing pattern.

Figure 167 shows a disassembled pistol which when put together is a very realistic briar pipe. It is carefully made with a rifled barrel that screws into the bowl and is marked SCULPTURED PUREX. The firing pin is cocked by pulling back a small button and turning it into a notch under the bowl. Pushing the button sideways out of the notch fires a .22 short cartridge.

The pistol in figure 168 appears to be nothing more than a pipe of unconventional design. This has a rifled steel barrel which is the mouth piece of the pipe. It is chambered for .22 LR cartridges and fitted to a bronze frame. The pipe bowl is ornamental wood. The hammer is the large knurled knob and the trigger is the button atop the frame. This is marked only COOL SMOKE.

Pistol pens and pistol pencils have been made in considerable numbers. Figure 169 illustrates a group of five. Each has a clip designed to hold the pistol upright in a pocket. Each is about 5″ long and fires a cartridge which to be loaded requires unscrewing the barrel. The barrels range from 5/8″ to 3½″ in length. Most guns of this type shoot .22's, but some have barrels that will chamber much heavier cartridges. These latter guns are in general intended only for gas cartridges. All are unmarked.

The heavy all metal pistol at the top of the group is of early construction. It is cocked by pulling the knob at the end straight back, and fired by pressing down the long trigger clip.

The second has the firing mechanism most commonly found

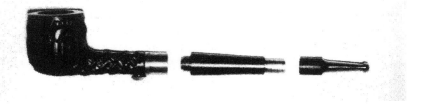

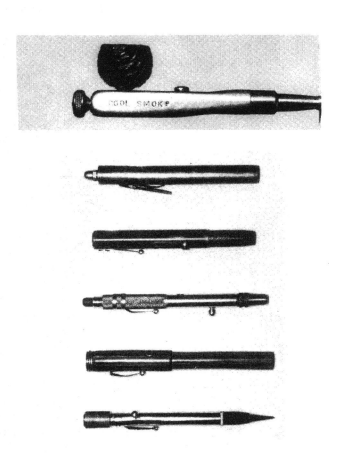

167. Pipe pistol/ Dr. W. R. Funderburg collection.

168. Pipe pistol/ Eddie Reider collection.

169. Group of pen and pencil pistols/ Eddie Reider collection.

on such pistols. The gun is cocked by pulling the striker back against spring pressure and slipping its button end sideways into a slot. It is fired by moving the button out of the slot.

The middle piece has a button trigger that moves out when the striker is pulled back. A slight pressure on the button will then fire the gun.

The fourth down looks like a modern plastic fountain pen. This is the best disguised of the lot. It is cocked by pulling back the metal top of the plastic cap and fired by pressure on a very small button in the cap.

These four pieces all fire from the end at the right in the illustration. None of the four actually incorporates either a pen or pencil.

The piece at the bottom has the muzzle at the left and an actual pencil at the right end.

The idea of attaching a pistol to a belt appealed to many inventors. Usually the belts were worn around the waist but sometimes they were held high on the chest. In some a short pistol barrel could be seen sticking out; in others the barrel was quite concealed. The most favored method of firing these contraptions was by pulling a string that ran up the sleeve, through the arm hole and down to the trigger.

How the percussion cap belt pistol, figures 170 and 171, operates may be seen at a glance. The oval iron plate is about 7″ long, and the pistol barrel protrudes about 1½″. In this gun the cord runs from the lock through a channel in the belt for a foot or more, before being carried up to the shoulder and down through a coat sleeve. A man ordered to put up his hands can grasp the weight and tighten the string as he raises his arms. A belt pistol such as this had no appeal as a work of art and it was unlikely to be treasured because of its history or associations. Once obsolete it was neglected, then discarded, soon it was rotted leather and scrap metal. Now this belt pistol is a scarce collector item.

The collector item shown in figures 172 and 173, though it is very modern, couldn't be scarcer. It is a German Nazi belt buckle pistol. Apparently several one-of-a-kind experimental models were made but only one example was made of the model intended for regular production. That particular piece, which bears serial #1 is the one pictured here.

It is about 2″ x 4″ and shoots cartridges similar to our .32 ACP

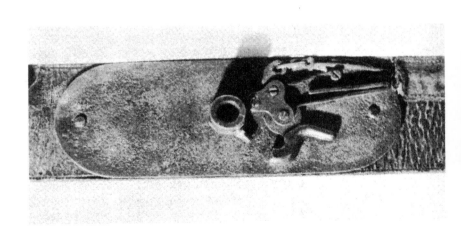

170. and 171. Belt pistol/ C. Stanley Jacob collection.

172. and 173. Belt buckle pistol/ Governor Gordon Persons collection.

cartridges. Normally the barrel group is folded down and concealed under the swastika and eagle ornamental cover. Putting this deadly four-shot battery in action may be done before the surprised victim can move. Two outside levers are squeezed simultaneously, thus releasing the barrels which force open the cover. Instantly the barrels are locked in place and ready to be fired by trigger pressure. The gun is not automatic. The shots may be fired one at a time at will, or the four triggers may be manipulated to fire two, three or all four shots together. Of the unblest guns that come sneakingly to kill this is probably the most efficient.

To the uninitiated, a gun collector's pulling a pepperbox from a bicycle handle bar is just as surprising as a magician's producing a rabbit from a boy's pocket. Handle bar pepperboxes were made in France and Belgium. They were probably all six-shot, double-action, using pin-fire cartridges of very small caliber, and were sold in pairs. Such a pair is illustrated in figures 174 and 175. The pepperbox shown detached was removed from the handle bar by a quick pull which left the rest of the handle bar grip an empty shell. The cylinder pin has a split end, and when compressed on being pushed back in place, will hold the two parts of the device together by friction. Some of these oddities had the two parts of each grip shaped alike, with straight ends, thus giving a better disguise.

In the previous chapter a Day's patent cane was described. Mr. Day made a number of all-metal truncheons, employing the same firing mechanisms used in the canes. There is no evidence Mr. Day had any success whatever in getting these truncheons approved for use by the London police. The example shown in figure 176 is a particularly desirable collector's specimen, being finely gilded and in a case with an extra barrel and a special powder flask. The illustration shows the gun having a short barrel screwed in place, and with a longer barrel of blunderbuss type in a separate compartment. A space for caps is provided in the sinister bird's-head grip. Of course, when used as a club, this piece has not the disadvantage of a lead pipe, which may bend on a tough skull.

There was also mentioned in the previous chapter a pepperbox fitted in a cane. Illustration 177 shows a pepperbox fitted in an umbrella. Except that this fires pin-fire instead of rim-fire car-

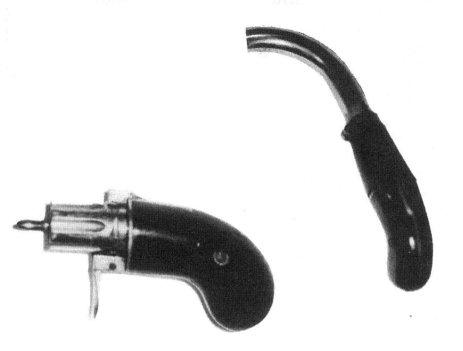

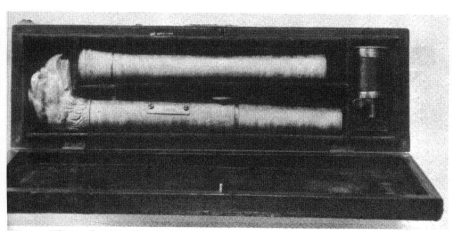

174. and 175. Handle bar pepperbox/ Osborne Klavestad collection.

176. Day's truncheon.

177. Umbrella pistol/ Eddie Reider collection.

tridges, and that it bears French markings, it is just like the cane pepperbox, but scarcer.

An early Spanish key pistol is shown in figure 178. The illustration is reprinted by permission from the forthcoming *Corpus and History of Hand Firearms* by Thomas T. Hoopes and William G. Renwick. The concealing of a pistol in a key, or of disguising a pistol as a key, has for centuries been a recognized but little used method of hiding a firearm. The miquelet lock on the piece shown is very interesting. Figure 179 is a view of the reverse of the lock. Notice the long lever attached to the top jaw of the cock and the unusual folding frizzen, or steel. The make-up of the lock seems well adapted to the close quarters provided. There is apparently no half-cock stud. Obviously, the barrel of the pistol is the stem and pin of the key.

Purses as repositories of concealed pistols are almost as common as pockets or holsters. However, we include here only pistols made to be fitted into specially made purses, or pistols made as integral parts of purses.

A good example of the former is shown in illustration 180. The bone-handled, single shot pistol is a very small and early European pin-fire. The case was made for no reason but to hold the gun.

An example of a pistol made as an integral part of a purse is to be seen in figures 181 and 182. This is the Frankenau "Combination Pocket-Book and Revolver", and is probably the only oddity of its type to be widely sold. It was patented both here and abroad—in the United States on November 6, 1877, patent #196,794. The British patent, #3375, dated September 5, 1877, refers to the invention as a "Revolver Purse". Both the British and American patent drawings show pepperbox construction, but the actual piece here pictured is a revolver with a very short barrel. It is double-action, six-shot, and fires 5 mm. pin-fire cartridges.

This unusual leather covered fabrication has a sheet metal center frame which divides it into two sections. As shown in the illustrations one section holds a compartmented change purse, while the other holds the revolver. The revolver section need be opened only for loading or unloading. It is not opened when the gun is fired. At one end of the frame is a pivoted gate to cover the barrel muzzle, and at the bottom is a well concealed folding

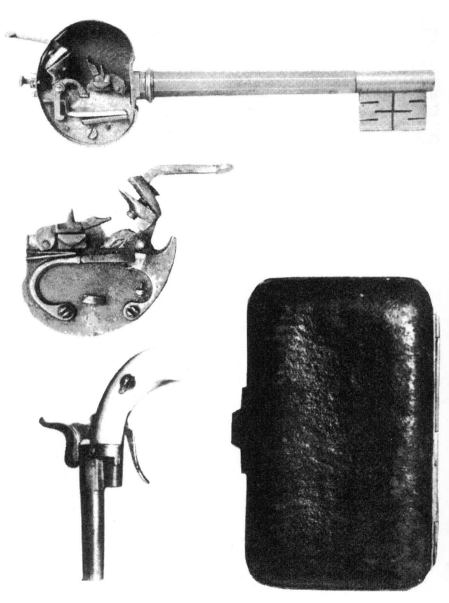

178. and 179. Key pistol/ Instituto de Valencia de Don Juan collection.

180. Pocket book pistol/ Frank R. Horner collection.

181. and 182. Frankenau purse pistol/ Gov. Gordon Persons collection.

trigger. To fire the gun it is only necessary to snap the trigger free and pull it. At the very beginning of the trigger pull an ingenious contrivance swings the pivoted gate or muzzle cover, out of the way. The closed purse-revolver is about 4″ x 2½″ x 1¼″. It is nearly the same in size and appearance as the case for the little pistol shown in figure 180.

Of all purse pistols, the combination of a flint pistol and a Scottish sporran is probably the top rarity. One such piece was, and perhaps still is, in the Museum of Edinburgh. Sir Walter Scott in his novel *Rob Roy,* describes one, the property of his hero, as ". . . a large leathern pouch, such as Highlanders of rank wear before them when in full dress, made of the skin of the sea otter, richly garnished with silver ornaments and studs." To quote further, " 'I advise no man to attempt opening this sporran till he has my secret', said Rob Roy; and then twisting one button in one direction, and another in another, pulling one stud upward, and pressing another downward, the mouth of the purse, which was bound with massive silver-plate, opened and gave admittance to his hand. He made me remark . . . that a small steel pistol was concealed within the purse, the trigger of which was connected with the mounting, and made part of the machinery, so that the weapon would certainly be discharged, and in all probability its contents lodged in the person of any one who, being unacquainted with the secret, should tamper with the lock which secured his treasure. 'This,' said he, touching the pistol—'this is the keeper of my privy purse.' "

Rob Roy would probably have traded the sporran and the privy purse for a modern sleeve pistol and a supply of ammunition. One such "Automatic concealed firearm for self defense", as E. B. Juhasz described his sleeve pistol in United States patent 1,726,228, granted August 27, 1929, is shown in figure 183. A glance at this illustration, and a brief examination of illustration 184, which shows part of the patent drawing, will probably make clear both how the gun is hidden and how it is fired. The pistol, which fires a .30 caliber center-fire cartridge, is fastened to a leather strap which has elastic bands to fit around the forearm. The barrel unscrews for loading. The gun pictured is cocked by pulling back a striker similar to the device commonly used on pen or pencil pistols. A wire or cord is run from the striker release to a ring on the middle finger. When the

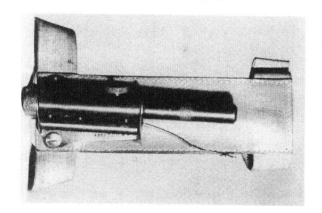

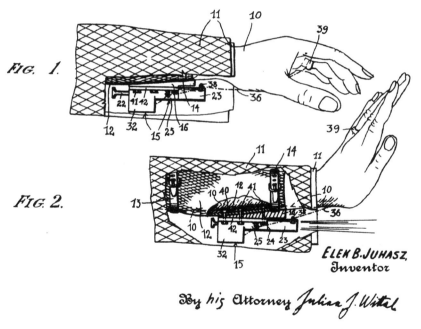

183. Sleeve pistol/ Eddie Reider collection.

184. Sleeve pistol patent drawing.

hand is flipped back the gun fires.

Many, many gadgets have been invented for attachment to firearms. There are lighting devices galore. Some illuminate the sights, some the target. Some throw a light beam when the trigger is pulled and are intended for use with an unloaded gun to show where a bullet would have gone.

A flashlight attached to a pistol, like a bayonet attached to a gun, hardly makes the firearm an oddity, but a revolver attached to a flashlight like a revolver attached to a bayonet, as in figure 31, is an oddity. It's the same old "Dog bites man—no news; man bites dog—news".

A flashlight with a revolver built in is pictured in figure 185. This is marked s. p. cottrell & son buffalo, n. y. and pat. u. s. jul. 10, 1923 and pat can. dec. 26, 1922. The flashlight is a conventional two cell type controlled by the usual sliding button. The 7-shot, .22 caliber revolver unit is screwed into and on the front part of the flashlight casing. It is double-action with a trigger that folds into the casing when not in use. An undated advertising folder furnished to me by Frank Wheeler, pictures one of these flashlight guns and states, "Aiming is unnecessary as the bullet must travel to center of the light. The most practical defense arm ever invented. Absolutely dependable. Price $12.00".

An all-metal German pistol, marked buco, and firing a center-fire cartridge of about .45 caliber, is shown in figure 186. This illustration shows the pistol ready to fire. To load, the large knurled cap is turned until two red marks are in line, when the cap will slip off. A cartridge is dropped in the barrel chamber. The cap is slipped back on, turned and locked so it forms a breech having at its inner center a raised projection which acts as a firing pin. The gun is cocked by pulling the barrel forward about an inch against heavy spring pressure, until it is held by a stud rising through an opening in the frame. The gun is fired by pressing down this stud.

When the military classes in Japan lost their feudal powers and their sword-carrying rights, in the 1870's, they may have become customers for concealed pistols. Illustration 187 shows a Japanese percussion pistol perfectly disguised, when sheathed, as a dagger which would be dangerous only in hand-to-hand fighting. The long hammer and the folding trigger fit perfectly in the narrow confines of the sheath. The piece is noteworthy be-

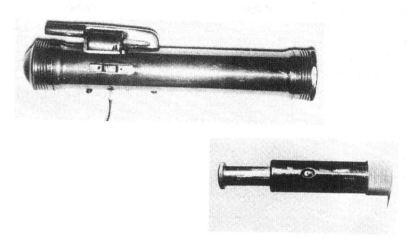

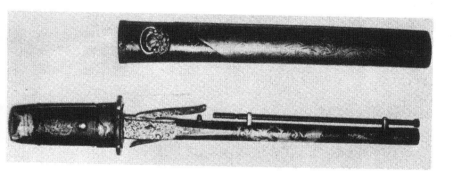

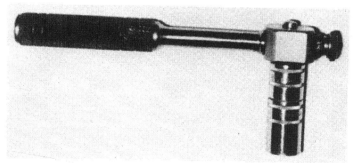

185. Flashlight pistol/ Dr. W. R. Funderburg collection.
186. "Buco" pistol/ Frank R. Horner collection.
187. Japanese pistol and sheath/ Eddie Reider collection.
188. Wrench pistol/ Governor Gordon Persons collection.

cause of its fine decoration. The sheath is covered partly with engraved metal and partly with shark skin, lacquered, colored and polished. The silver dragon inlaid in the barrel is very artistically done.

A wrench pistol of uncertain origin but probably of World War II vintage is pictured in figure 188. It is an American all-steel socket or box wrench, size $2\frac{1}{32}$", converted to a single-shot pistol using some special center-fire cartridge of about .26 caliber. The handle of the wrench becomes the barrel of the pistol, and the socket head becomes the pistol grip. The knurled part of the wrench handle may be unscrewed to load a cartridge. The cartridge may be fired after pulling the round projection which is the hammer, and pressing with the thumb the button on top which is the trigger. Probably very few of these wrench pistols were made.

Illustrations 189 and 190 show two small single-shot pistols such as were sometimes carried by men on special and hazardous assignments in World War II. Neither pistol is marked. One, figure 189, of bright steel, is reportedly German and can be unscrewed for reloading. The other, painted green, is American made, and an issue item to small numbers of o. s. s. men. This latter pistol, officially known as the OSS Stinger, is single-shot in the strictest sense—it can't be reloaded. It is welded in the middle, after being loaded. Either pistol is fired by release of the hook-shaped wire at the breech end. On the American piece the safety lever, like a pencil clip, is held by a plastic ring which must be slipped off before firing.

In figures 191 and 192 are two views of a primitive percussion cap pepperbox in the form of a whiskey cask made of German silver. The cask headings, each of which has a swivel resembling a carrying ring attached, hide the hammer at one end, and the barrel muzzles at the other end. A pull on one of the swivels will cock the gun. A twist of the other swivel will drop a small plate and disclose a barrel muzzle, as in figure 192. The end bands—the hoops that bind the staves—are free to turn, and so permit manual rotation of the pepperbox cylinder and successive firing of nine shots. The trigger is the small button sticking out from one of the hoops.

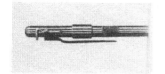

189. Metal pistol—3½″ overall/ Eddie Reider collection.

190. Metal pistol/ George R. Numrich, Jr. collection.

191. and 192. Primitive pepperbox/ Anthony Fidd, Jr. collection.

Chapter 9

SUPERPOSED LOADS

It happened many times in the days of cap lock muskets that a soldier in battle would not notice if his musket misfired. In case of an unnoticed misfire, he might ram a second charge on top of the first. The barrel then, by mistake, had superposed loads.

The guns with which this chapter is concerned are not those muskets unintentionally charged with superposed loads. The guns here considered are those repeaters with barrels purposely charged with superposed loads.

Of all the ideas for producing multishot firearms the scheme of superimposing loads in one barrel is probably the oldest, the most discredited, the most frequently recurring, and also the most readily accepted as new.

Superposed load guns were of two types, widely different in operation.

In one type the operator had no control of the interval between shots; he could not stop the firing once he had started it. Let's call this kind the Roman candle type. It was charged like a Roman candle, one load on top of another; it also functioned like a Roman candle in that it was self-acting in firing.

Let's call the other kind the controlled type. This, too, was charged with one load on top of another, but the operator had control of the interval between shots. It might have one movable lock or several fixed locks. Each shot would be fired by trigger pull, presumably when the operator felt he had the proper aim.

With the Roman candle type the best the operator could do after the first shot, was to estimate when the self-firing gun would fire its next shot, and try to have the gun properly aimed at that time.

In one form of Roman candle gun the foremost charge was set off by a fuse lighted at the gun muzzle, as a fireworks candle is set off. In the other form the firing was started by gunlock ignition through a touch hole. Roman candle guns were made at least as early as the 17th century, and as late as the 19th, using wheel lock, flintlock and cap lock ignition, but examples of any such guns are extremely scarce. In fact, no American gun with the name Chambers or Kesling on it is known to be still in existence. Joseph Chambers, in flintlock days, and George Kesling, in cap lock days, were probably the only American inventors of Roman candle guns. The Kesling is known to have been a Roman candle type because the Kesling patent is clear on that point. Final proof that the Chambers was of Roman candle ignition came this year with the discovery by John C. McMurray of an early 19th century description of the Chambers invention. More of the Chambers and the Kesling guns later, and of a pistol that might be of Chambers construction.

We do not know just how far back the idea of self-igniting cartridges goes. It would seem that in 1682 Charles Cardiff had the idea "which hitherto by none but himselfe hath been invented or knowne." The quotation is from British Patent #216, granted to "our trusty and wellbeloved Charles Cardiff, Gentleman", by Charles II. The patent described the invention as "an Expedient with Security to make Musketts, Carbines, Pistolls, or any other small Fire Armes to Discharge twice, thrice, or more severall and distincte Shotts in a Singell Barrell and Locke with once Primeing . . .". It further stated that "the Mistery (is) in the Charge."

Mr. Cardiff's patent implied that double locks could be used and that one or more shots could be reserved "till occasion offer." It would seem Mr. Cardiff had in mind two fixed locks, with a separate touch hole for each, the forward one to fire a Roman candle series of charges, and the rear one to fire one or more charges after the series of explosions started by the forward lock was completed. The wording of the patent is indefinite and we can not be completely sure that Mr. Cardiff planned to insert a solid rather than a perforated bullet somewhere in a series of superposed loads so as to stop the Roman candle effect and to permit resumption of firing by means of another lock.

A very rare and fine German piece is shown in figure 193. This most remarkable gun is capable of doing everything we assume Mr. Cardiff's double-lock gun may have been capable of doing, and it appears to antedate Mr. Cardiff's patent. No maker's name is on it, but the Nuremberg mark is clear.

As illustration 193 shows, there are two locks, the forward being a conventional wheel lock, and the rear an unusual combination wheel lock-matchlock. There is but one trigger.

The gun may be used as a single-shot, employing the rear lock only, or it may be charged with sixteen superposed loads so that the first pull of the trigger will release the wheel on the forward lock and fire nine Roman candle charges, a second pull will release the wheel on the rear lock and set off six more such charges, and finally a third pull will fire the one remaining shot.

A safety catch which prevents movement of the wheel on the rear lock at the first trigger pull must be released, after the first series of nine shots, before the second series of six shots can be discharged. To fire the final shot by the third trigger pull it is necessary either again to span the wheel of the rear lock, or to use the match ignition.

The trigger is connected to the forward lock by a wire running through the frame. When the trigger is pulled the priming powder is ignited and fire goes from the pan directly through a touch hole to the foremost powder charge. If the gun be properly loaded the first shot will be followed by eight more self-acting and unpreventable discharges going off in quick succession.

The ignition of the first of the six shots in the second series requires that a train of priming powder be laid from the pan of the rear lock to a touch hole located some six or more inches frontward. A tube is provided that runs under the lockplate and along the barrel. This tube is detachable so it may be readily filled with the flash powder and is held to the barrel by a clip.

After the firing of both series of Roman candle shots the gun remains a loaded single-shot weapon. For the final shot the pan of the rear lock must be reprimed, and a sliding gate between the pan and a rearmost touch hole moved aside. The shot may

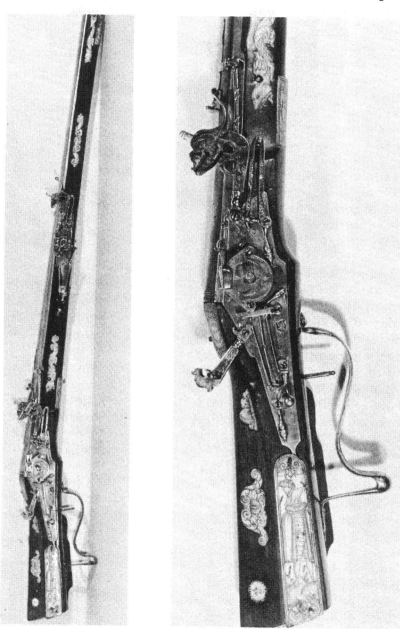

193. and 194. Wheel lock gun/ Frank E. Bivens, Jr. collection.

then be set off either by the matchlock or the wheel lock. Whether pressure on the trigger will send the spanned wheel spinning or move a lighted match into the pan, depends on how a lever on the side of the lock is set.

A close-up of the remarkable rear lock is shown in figure 194.

No original bullets for this gun exist, but charges such as were used in the Chambers gun, or even combustible cartridges such as were used in the Danish espingoles, could be successfully used in it. As in the Kesling gun (which along with the espingoles and the Chambers guns will be described shortly) the first bullet to be loaded would be solid. The seventh and sixteenth bullets, in order of loading, would also be solid.

It is perhaps well to depart at this time from a chronological order, so the espingole cartridges may be described. The espingoles were multiple barrel weapons used by Danish military forces, chiefly the Navy. An early report made in 1842 by the Chief of Naval Ordnance of Denmark reported that the guns could not be used freehand, and went on to say, ". . . the espingole must have a support and may thus be used only at places adapted for the purpose . . ." and ". . . when ignition has taken place the shooting cannot be stopped. The loading of the espingole can be performed only by trained people; it must be executed with the greatest care, requires a lot of appliances, takes up much time, and consequently cannot be done during a battle." Improvements were made, the early smooth bore barrels were later rifled, and the espingoles were kept in use in quantity for another thirty years. The novelty of these guns was in their combustible paper cartridges. Each cartridge had its bullet with a hole bored longitudinally through the center. This hole contained a slow burning fuse. When the fuse in the foremost cartridge was lighted by the operator, the charge would shortly explode and at the same time ignite the fuse in the next cartridge. From then on the explosions were automatic. The intervals between shots which gave the operator time to take aim were determined by the burning speed of the train of slow burning powder, or fuse.

The two important improvements in the espingole, the rifling of the barrels and the fully developed cartridges, came about 1850.

Figure 195 reproduces illustration #332 from Thierbach's

Geschichtliche Entwickelung der Handfeuerwaffen. This is a Roman candle type using flintlock ignition and is dated by Thierbach as circa 1780. The gun is a breech loader, taking a long cartridge into which loads had been superposed like those in the Danish espingole. Thierbach states that guns functioning like the 1780 flintlock were known even before 1780 in Denmark.

A pistol that may have been made on an American patent granted Joseph Chambers on March 23, 1813, is shown in figure 196. The Chambers patent is one of which only the briefest of records remained after the 1836 Patent Office fire. The Patent Office records show Mr. Chambers' patent was for a repeating gun, but these records give no hint of either the mechanism or the method of operation. Correspondence and other documents of the time of the War of 1812 have established that shoulder guns, swivel guns, and probably pistols were manufactured on the Chambers principle. This material has convinced students that the guns used superposed loads.

This very interesting pistol, figure 196, is one of a pair, with English barrels, but with American locks and stocks. The pistols were made in Philadelphia, by Peloux, an early nineteenth century maker of very fine pistols, rifles and shotguns, both flintlock and cap lock. There is no marking to indicate the guns were made under the Chambers patent, and there is no evidence that Peloux knew anything about the Chambers guns, though Chambers guns were surely made in Philadelphia by Tryon. The two Philadelphia makers, Tryon and Peloux, were contemporaneous.

The lock on this pistol is placed 3½″ forward of the position it would be in if the touch hole were in the normal position for a single-shot pistol. This construction would allow three normal charges to be rammed in the barrel, with the touch hole opposite the powder in the foremost charge. With perforated bullets such as were used in the Chambers guns, the pistol might well be made to shoot like a Roman candle. A normal flintlock with its mainspring on the inside could hardly be fitted so far forward on the stock. There is not enough wood in the forestock for proper inletting of such a lock. The lock on this pistol is of special construction, with its mainspring on the outside, so it can be secured in a position that would be unaccountable in a single-shot pistol.

One accepted description of the Chambers gun stated, "by a

single operation of the trigger it will discharge several loads in succession . . . with space between sufficient to take another aim." This Peloux pistol, if loaded with proper cartridges having perforated bullets, would seem able to meet these stated conditions.

Doubts have been expressed by some collectors that the Chambers guns manufactured by Tryon had Roman candle ignition rather than controlled type with a sliding lock. There were two reasons for these doubts. One was the absence of data as to the charges used. The other was the vagueness of a reference in an early document to a "foremost touch hole" in the Chambers gun. It was thought by some that "foremost touch hole" must indicate a system of ignition like that on the later Jennings flintlock, though the early Cardiff gun may well have been, and the later Kesling surely was, a Roman candle type with a "foremost touch hole".

As has been previously mentioned, John C. McMurray has located an early description of a Chambers gun which fills the gap in our knowledge and fully proves the gun was a true Roman candle firearm. It is hoped that complete details of Mr. McMurray's research will be published by him either before or soon after this writing is in print. The early 19th century statement described the bullet used as being a cylinder pierced with a hole in the center which contained a fuse composition. The description stated that charges of powder, and cylinders, were loaded alternately, and that the lock was placed opposite the last charge —which would be opposite that "foremost touch hole"—so that when that charge was fired "the fire communicates successively through the cylinders."

The Kesling gun, for which U. S. patent #15,041 was granted June 3, 1856, to Mr. George Kesling of Lebanon, Ohio, fired both a series of perforated-bullet cartridges and one solid-bullet cartridge. The solid bullet stopped the Roman candle effect and kept one shot in reserve to be fired at pleasure by a second lock. Mr. Kesling stated he knew of the previous use of superposed charges having perforated bullets and he claimed as new only the use of a series of vents designed to permit the escape of trapped air and to allow the charges to be "rammed home airtight." Figure 197 is a reproduction of the patent drawing. It shows a gun having twelve loads, using one cartridge with a

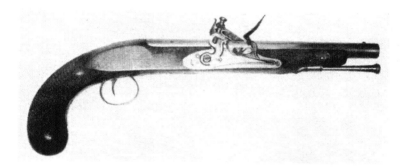

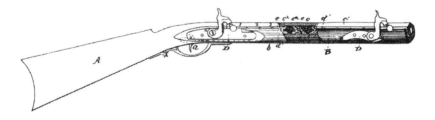

195. Illustration from Thierbach's *Die Geschichtliche Entwickelung der Handfeuerwaffen.*

196. Peloux pistol/ Sam E. Smith collection.

197. Kesling patent drawing.

solid bullet on which were superposed eleven cartridges of the Danish espingole type. Of the twelve vents only two, the first and the last, were touch holes for the locks. The ten in between were to permit escape of air, and to permit powder to be pricked into the barrel in case a charge was "not properly introduced." It can be seen that after eleven Roman candle shots were discharged, one shot remained to be fired when the operator desired to raise the rear hammer and again press the trigger.

Examples of superposed load guns which permit controlled firing are frequently seen. Some of the many types are of course very much scarcer than others, but they are not completely non-existent, as the "lost Chambers gun" seems to be.

The rifles made on the 1821 Isaiah Jennings patent are among the more scarce of the controlled type superposed load guns. Though the 1821 patent specifications for the Jennings rifle were lost in the same fire that destroyed the specifications for the 1813 Chambers gun, there is no doubt about the mechanism of the Jennings. One of the repeaters bearing the Jennings name and having the sliding flintlock was in the U. S. Cartridge Company collection.

About 1828 a New York State maker, Reuben Ellis, made military rifles under contract on the Jennings principle. Perhaps similar pieces were made, or assembled, by other makers. One of these rifles, bearing U. S. inspection and property marks, and probably made by Ellis, is shown in illustration 198. The gun is a "common rifle" of the 1819 model, equipped with a sliding flintlock and having a barrel with four touch holes. The lock has an attached magazine that automatically supplies priming powder to the flash pan when the hammer is cocked. There are covers for three touch holes—none is needed for the foremost touch hole. These covers also index the lock. The illustration shows the gun ready to fire its second shot. The first shot has been fired, the forward vent cover thrown up, the lock drawn back until its pan is opposite the second vent, the hammer cocked. Pressure on the trigger will raise a bar that is sufficiently long to release the sear, regardless of where the sear has been placed by movement of the lock.

Another very interesting example of a sliding lock gun is illustrated in figure 199. This 4-shot flint pistol is marked JOVER & BELTON, LONDON. The curious back-striking lock will slide along

198. Jennings rifle/ John C. McMurray collection.

199. Jover & Belton pistol—16½" overall/ Pitt Rivers Museum collection, University of Oxford.

the barrel and be held at one-after-another of the four touch holes. Between shots, the lock is drawn to the next touch hole, the hammer is cocked, the frizzen pressed down, and the revolving pan primed. Pressing down the small lever under the pan turns the pan and primes it.

Both Pollard and George agree that Jover & Belton, who made this pistol, were in business in London in 1786. It may be assumed the firm operated under this name for a short time only, and that the pistol illustrated was made well before either the American Roman candle or sliding-lock designs of the early 19th century.

The records of the Continental Congress show that in 1777 an order was approved for construction under the direction of Joseph Belton of 100 muskets "which will discharge eight rounds with once loading." It is unknown what the guns were like or if any were made, other than a single example surely exhibited by Joseph Belton. We have no reason to assume there is more than coincidence in the fact the name Belton appears as maker of both the 1777 American repeater and the 1786 English repeater. The name is not uncommon.

The controlled-fire types of superposed load guns also included various forms having fixed, rather than movable, locks.

Such guns having a separate lock and touch hole for each load were made in matchlock and wheel lock, as well as in the later flintlock and cap lock. At least one double loading gun was produced which fired the forward charge with a wheel lock and the rear charge with a flintlock, both locks being on the same lockplate and fired by the same trigger. The flintlock employed a dog safety to prevent the fall of the flint hammer when the trigger released the spanned wheel lock.

A very good example of a superposed load flintlock pistol using two locks is the one of a pair shown in figure 200. This is a very simple arrangement of two locks on a single lockplate, with a touch hole lined up with each pan. On this piece one trigger suffices for both locks. The gun is shown with the forward lock ready to fire when the trigger is pressed. After that the rear hammer may be drawn back to full cock and the trigger pressed again for a second shot.

Guns on this style with two side locks, one in advance of the other, continued to appear sporadically as long as muzzle-loaders

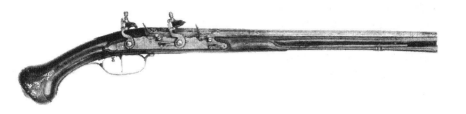

200. Superposed load pistol—23″ overall/ Joseph Kindig, Jr. collection.

201. Superposed load pistol/ Dr. W. R. Funderburg collection.

were in demand. In fact, at the end of the cap lock era double-barrel superposed load shotguns were produced in Belgium with two right-hand and two left-hand locks. A gun with two barrels was not put completely out of action by a single misfire, as a single-barrel gun might be. The dread of misfires was reason enough for the lack of sustained enthusiasm for any of the superposed load guns.

The two-shot pistol shown in illustration 201 has one barrel with two locks operated by a single trigger. With both hammers cocked, trigger pressure will drop the right hammer. A second pressure will drop the left hammer. The vent leading to the forward charge runs from the pan of the right lock through a channel in the thickened and widened lockplate until it reaches the forward touch hole.

It is worth noting here that a single trigger, one barrel gun having a right-hand lock directly opposite a left-hand lock is not necessarily two-shot. Some guns of that construction are single-shot. The touch holes both lead to the same powder charge. The hammers fall together and lessen the chance of a misfire. See illustrations 256 and 257.

Firing superposed loads by sending the fire for the forward charge through a channel that by-passed the rear charge became the most widely used system even though this use of a long channel caused excessive fouling. A gun on this system might have two locks, like the one already shown in illustration 201, or it might have but one lock, like figure 202, or figure 203.

Figure 202 is a Queen Anne pistol, marked T. GIBSON, LONDON. This has a very unusual mechanism for firing its two superposed loads, making use of a two-part flash pan. A channel from the upper part leads to the forward charge, while a vent in the lower part goes directly to the rear charge. The rounded end of the lever fastened to the pan is pointed toward the muzzle when priming the pan. To prepare for the first shot the lever is turned back, thereby covering the lower part of the pan and putting part of the powder in the upper level and part in the lower level. For the second shot the lever is moved back to its original position, so the scraping flint will ignite the powder in the now uncovered lower level.

Another similar but less complicated pistol firing two superposed loads with one lock is pictured in figure 203. This is one of

202. Gibson pistol—13½″ overall/ Joseph Kindig, Jr. collection.

203. Richards pistol/ Joseph Kindig, Jr. collection.

204. Mould rifle/ Photograph courtesy Harold G. Young.

a pair, also English, and is marked RICHARDS, STRAND, LONDON. Again there are two pans one above the other. The floor of the top pan is the cover of the lower pan. After sparks have ignited the priming powder in the upper pan, and fired the forward charge, the previously primed lower pan may be uncovered by pulling back a sliding lever on the left, not visible in the illustration.

The illustrations that follow in this chapter will all be of percussion cap pieces, and all will be of the controlled-fire type. Some, like the pocket model Lindsay pistols and the 10-shot Walch revolvers, exist in considerable numbers. The remainder range from very scarce to unique, and from very plain to a work of art by a master gunsmith.

Illustration 204 is of an English rifle made under a British patent of February 19, 1825, granted to Jacob Mould. This is a four-shot with a sliding lock. Mr. Mould specified ". . . a series of touch-holes along the barrel or breech of any fire-arm, and in the application thereto of a sliding or other adjusting lock, to act by percussion or otherwise, whereby any number of charges not exceeding the number of touch-holes may be inserted in the barrel at one time and fired successively".

On February 27, 1855, Daniel B. Neal, of Mount Gilead, Ohio, obtained United States patent #12,440 for a "Double-Shooting One-Barrel Fire-arm". Illustration 205 shows the patent model with the lock in the position it would be after firing the first shot. The nose of the elongated hammer has struck the top of a false hammer, driving the nose of that false hammer hard against the forward cone. When the true hammer is now again cocked, the hinged false hammer may be thrust aside by pressing forward on the front trigger. A pull on the conventional rear trigger will this time let the true hammer strike the cap on the rear cone, the false hammer no longer intervening.

On September 25, 1855, Frederick Beerstecher, of Philadelphia, Pennsylvania, obtained United States patent #13,592, covering the peculiar lock on the pistol shown in figure 206. This pistol, of the shape made famous by Henry Deringer, is marked on the lockplate F. BEERSTECHER'S PATENT 1855 and on the barrel LEWISBURG, PA and PATENT 1855. Mr. Beerstecher's invention eliminated the false hammer of the pistol patented seven months earlier by Mr. Neal, and substituted a supplementary hinged

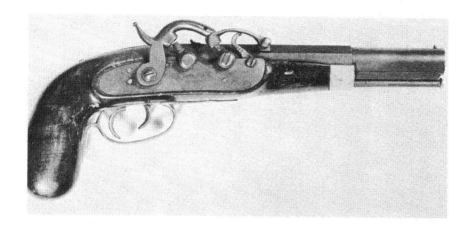

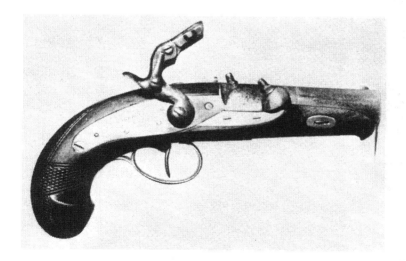

205. Neal pistol/ Smithsonian Institution collection.

206. Beerstecher pistol—6¾" overall/ Calvin Hetrick collection.

hammer nose. The illustration shows Mr. Beerstecher's patented hammer cocked and with its hinged extension in position to reach the forward nipple when the trigger is pulled. If the cocked hammer were now to have the extension pressed down, this extension would veer to the right so as to clear the barrel and rest alongside it on descent. At the left of the solid part of the hammer head and integral with it, is a striking nose that will reach the rear nipple when, and only when, the pistol is fired with the hinged extension turned down.

Still another idea for firing two superposed loads is shown in figure 207. This is French and is probably the simplest method ever devised to convert a single-shot gun into a two-shot. The lock requires no more than the changing of the regulation hammer to the two-headed hammer illustrated. When the trigger is pulled with the screw of the rear hammer nose drawn back as in the illustration, only the front hammer strikes its nipple. For the second shot the screw is turned fully in so the rear hammer nose will reach its nipple.

The conversion of a single-shot pistol to the bizarre four-shot in figure 208 was the work of an unknown and uninhibited gunsmith. The unmarked pistol he converted is possibly a Confederate piece. The gun is as unconventional in operation as in appearance. Under the barrel is a spindle that is turned by a ratchet device actuated by the ring trigger. Four studs on this spindle engage the hammers one after another. After one trigger pull raises a hammer, the next pull releases that hammer. With the spindle properly set to cock the foremost hammer, eight successive trigger pulls will empty the gun and put the spindle back in position to raise the foremost hammer again. The illustration shows the gun cocked for the second shot.

We come now to the Lindsay "Double Shooting Fire Arms" of which well over a thousand each of pistols and muskets were manufactured.

Except for the contemporaneous Walch revolvers, we find the Lindsay muskets and the Lindsay pistols the only American superposed load guns well known to collectors. The activities and the fortunes of the two men, John Walch, who patented the revolver, and John Lindsay, who patented the pistol, were intermixed. The dates of both the Walch patent and the Lindsay patent appeared on second model Lindsay pistols, while 10-

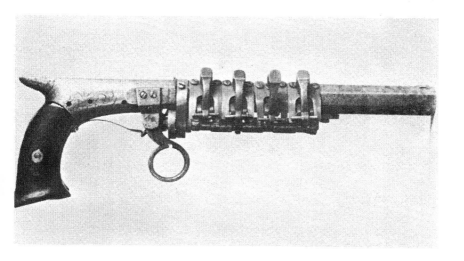

207. French carbine/ Harold G. Young collection.

208. Four-shot conversion—12″ overall/ Dr. J. S. Golden, Jr. collection.

shot Walch revolvers used the trigger patented by Lindsay. One existing Lindsay pistol is known to be marked "Walch Fire Arms Co." as well as "Lindsay's Young America". Probably all Walch revolvers bore the Walch name, and none bore the Lindsay name, but the 10-shot Walch revolvers were referred to in advertising and press comments as Lindsay products called "Ten-Shooters".

The March 1, 1862, issue of *Harper's Weekly* carried an advertisement referring to "Lindsay's New Fire-Arms" as "The most effective and reliable weapons in use".

It is interesting to notice that unqualified superlatives were used as freely then as now, though without audible frenzy. The same page of that 1862 Harper's had an advertisement describing Elliot's Pocket Revolver as "The most compact and powerful Pocket Revolver ever made", and also an advertisement stating the Army pronounced Prescott's Cartridge Revolvers, "the best and most effective weapons in use".

Both the Elliot revolver (a Remington product) and the Prescott·revolver used rim-fire cartridges. Lindsay was competing against these breechloaders with a muzzle-loader. Mr. Lindsay recognized the inherent superiority of the self-contained cartridges. He went so far as to experiment with a double-loading breechloader but he did not get beyond the point of patenting a double-loaded pin-fire cartridge.

Two examples of the first type Lindsay pistols are shown in figure 209. Each has two hammers and two stub triggers. With both hammers cocked the first trigger squeeze drops the right hammer and sends fire from the detonated cap through a channel to the forward charge. Another squeeze and the left trigger releases the left hammer. Of these rarely found two-trigger Lindsays the lower one is the more uncommon. The variation is in the shape of the barrel and in the fact two screws instead of one are used in the lower pistol to attach the barrel to the frame. Both guns are stamped LINDSAY'S YOUNG AMERICA and PATENT APD. FOR. The upper bears serial 145 and the lower serial 157.

Though these two-trigger pistols are marked "Patent applied for" Mr. Lindsay did not obtain a patent for them. He did, on October 9, 1860, obtain U. S. patent #30,332 for his single-trigger pistol, which we call the second model. It is probable that

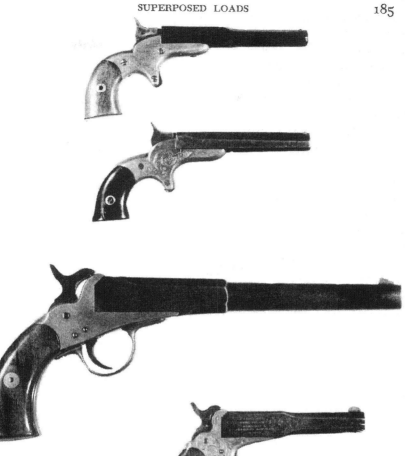

209. First type Lindsay pistols/ Sam E. Smith collection.

210. Later type Lindsay pistols/ Sam E. Smith collection.
Photographs courtesy *The Gun Collector.*

when Mr. Lindsay invented his single-trigger model he was permitted to withdraw an earlier application for a patent on his two-trigger model. Two types of this second model pistol are illustrated in figure 210. The stub-trigger pocket type, which was referred to in advertisements either as "Young America" or "Double Deringer", is slightly smaller than the first model. It differs from the first model in two major aspects: it has but one trigger, and it has nipples set at an angle of 45° to the barrel bore. It is the type most frequently seen. The particular piece illustrated bears serial #952 and is marked LINDSAY'S YOUNG AMERICA MAN'F'D BY J. P. LINDSAY MAN'F'G CO. NEW YORK.

Lindsay firearms were manufactured both in Naugatuck and New Haven, Connecticut. Mr. Lindsay gave New York as his address in his patent application, but it is not known that any of his firearms were actually manufactured there. The practice of stamping a metropolitan address, such as New York or London, on products manufactured elsewhere was not uncommon.

The large single-trigger pistol at the top of illustration 210 is the type called the Army model by collectors and the Navy model by Lindsay. It is like the pocket type, except in size and in the fact it has a conventional trigger guard.

The large model was .44 caliber, or more. The other Lindsay pistols were about .40 caliber. Some Lindsay pistols were rifled and some were not. The pistol bullet usually had two nearly spherical ends, like the weights of a dumbbell, connected with a short bar. It looked like a dumbbell. The space around the connecting bar was to be filled with grease before the bullet was rammed down the barrel, either end first. The grease helped keep the barrel clean and also prevented fire from the forward charge escaping around the bullet of the rear charge and exploding that. The little brass molds made to cast these bullets are quite scarce.

Neither the Army nor the Navy seems to have been interested in the large Lindsay pistol, but the Army did contract for, accept delivery of, and pay for one thousand Lindsay muskets at $25.00 each. It is doubtful that any of these Rifle Muskets, as they were called, saw combat duty. In initial tests where directions were carefully followed, the guns performed satisfactorily. Later tests showed the guns fouled badly, and that fire would leak back around the rear bullet. The statement, "Fire *cannot* pass back to rear charge, if the *grooves* in the ball are properly *filled with lubrication, and balls thoroughly rammed home"*, was probably true, but it is equally true that soldiers on the battle-field may neglect the proper filling with lubricant and the proper seating of the bullets.

The italics in that quotation are Mr. Lindsay's. The sentence quoted is the last one on the reproduced front page, illustration 211, of a two-leaf descriptive folder put out by Lindsay Fire Arms Co., New Haven, Connecticut. The illustration shows the musket bullets are not of the dumbbell type used in Lindsay pistols. It also shows the interior of the patented lock. If both hammers were cocked the rear charge could not be fired inadvertently until the right hammer was dropped. Still, the left hammer could be cocked singly to fire the rear charge when the front charge was yet unfired.

Mr. Lindsay disapproved firing both shots at once, but he affirmed that such firing could be done safely in either the pistol or the long gun. However, the possibility of unintentional firing of both charges at once was probably enough in itself to get the guns condemned for military use.

An advertisement picturing the "Double Deringer" and the "Ten-Shooter", but mentioning no other firearms was issued by "J. P. Lindsay Manufg Co.", Naugatuck, Connecticut. The later folder issued by "Lindsay Fire Arms Co.", New Haven, Connecticut, deals exclusively with the musket except for the mere naming of other types of firearms "constructed upon the same principle". These are listed as, Shot Guns, Sporting Rifles, Navy Pistols and Pocket Pistols. Revolvers are not mentioned.

The close association of John Lindsay and John Walch is evident from a statement made by a patent attorney at the time he argued, successfully, for the granting of Lindsay's patent, which was at first rejected as being in conflict with Walch's patent. Attorney Fitzgerald stated that all Walch revolvers had been made under the immediate care and inspection of Mr. Lindsay.

The very first of the Walch revolvers were single-trigger, made ". . . with the double hammers acted on by one trigger . . ." in conformity with the patent granted John Walch, February 8, 1859, U. S. Patent #22,905. The next group of Walch revolvers were two-trigger using the construction found on the early Lind-

LINDSAY'S PATENT
Double Shooting Fire Arms

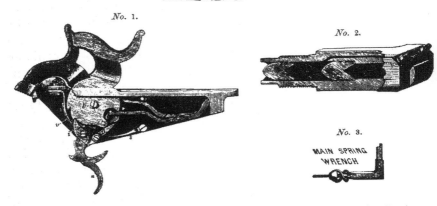

No. 1.

No. 2.

No. 3.

MAIN SPRING
WRENCH

Cut No. 1 represents interior of Lock, *b b* Hammers, *e e* Main Spring, *i i* Scears, *v v* Scear Springs, *r* Screw, which holds *scear spring* and *cap* in place, *n* Trigger, *o* Detent, which *prevents* both hammers falling by a *single* pull of the trigger, *s* Detent Spring, *t* Main Spring *Wrench* hole.

Cut No. 2 represents the inner section of breech, with two charges in position.

GENERAL FORMATION. The double lock is inserted into the stock directly in *rear* of barrel. The barrel breach is provided with *two* cones and *two* vents, which communicate with the *separate* charges of powder—the *right* one with *front* charge, the *left* one with *rear* charge. Both charges are loaded into, and fired from *one* barrel separately. By these simple means a *double gun* is obtained *without* necessary *additional weight* above a single barrel arm.

CONSTRUCTION. The *bottom* of the bore is *decreased* in size, forming a chamber. (See cut No. 2.) This *chamber* receives *powder only from one* cartridge. The *rear* or first ball rests upon the edges of this chamber, completely *sealing up the powder* in the chamber. Upon this *rear ball* the *second* charge of *powder* and ball rests. The vent to the *front* charge passes from *right* hand cone through the metal to a point *between* the balls. The vent to the rear charge passes from left hand cone directly into small chamber.

AMMUNITION used should *always* be the *regular Springfield paper pressed ball* cartridge. *Full size* for caliber $^{58}/_{100}$. *Grooves* in ball should be *filled* with lubrication. Fire *cannot* pass back to rear charge, if the *grooves* in the ball are properly *filled with lubrication, and balls thoroughly "rammed home."*

211. Lindsay instruction sheet.

say pistols. The last of the Walch revolvers were single-trigger, of the same construction found on the second model Lindsay pistols.

Mr. Walch's first application for a patent to cover firing of superposed loads by the use of two hammers and one trigger was too far-reaching and was rejected because the patent granted Johnson Marsh on July 1, 1836, anticipated Mr. Walch's claims. When Mr. Walch limited his claims to revolvers he received his patent. Figure 212 is a reproduction of the drawing for the Johnson Marsh invention. No printed specification is available. The drawing shows a pistol with pill lock ignition. The invention's name, as printed on the patent drawing, is "Double Shot Gun."

The large, early one-trigger Walch revolvers are of two types, both extremely scarce. The very first of these were like the patent model illustrated in figure 213. These had a very long hammer to reach the row of nipples set well forward in the cylinder. The short hammer made to strike the caps on the row of nipples at the back of the cylinder "passes through an opening of the forward hammer", as Mr. Walch explained the action. The rest of the large early one-trigger Walch revolvers, one of which is shown in figure 214, had the hammers side by side, with the cones all placed at the rear of the cylinder. Whereas on the very first type the long hammer itself bypassed the rear charge, on this type the usual long channel was required to lead the fire from the cap around the rear charge to the forward charge. In appearance this last-mentioned type was like the later two-trigger model, except it lacked the hump on the grip, and of course lacked the second trigger.

Unless pressure on the trigger of the early one-trigger model was stopped right after the forward charge was fired, the next shot would follow instantly.

So, the two-trigger model shown at the top in illustration 215 was designed to correct that bad feature—to lessen the possibility the shooter could not prevent the unintentional firing of the second charge. For the novice in the use of a revolver the problem was still not solved. He would be apt to pull hard on the forward trigger and fail to stop the pressure before pressing back the second trigger.

The two smaller revolvers in the group of three, illustration 215, are 10-shot. One has a brass frame and one an iron frame.

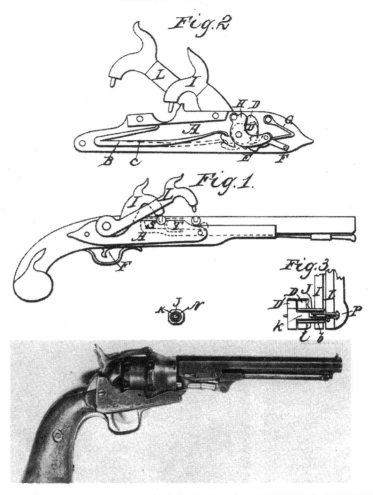

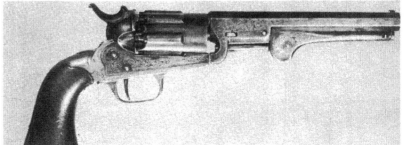

212. J. Marsh patent drawing.
213. Twelve-shot Walch/ Smithsonian Institution collection.
214. Twelve-shot Walch/ Henry M. Stewart collection.

215. Twelve-shot and ten-shot Walch revolvers/ Sam E. Smith collection.
Photograph courtesy *The Gun Collector*.

This Ten-Shooter was the last model Walch and was produced in much larger quantities than the earlier large models, which were all probably iron frame and 12-shot.

The Ten-Shooter used the single-trigger construction of the Lindsay patent, which was a great improvement over that patented by Walch. It was very much more nearly foolproof in the hands of an inexperienced shooter because the construction required release of the trigger after firing one shot before firing another. One continuous pull would not cause two discharges.

Collectors of art in firearms give high praise to many pieces bearing the name Le Page. The illustrations that conclude this chapter are of two fine examples of Le Page guns using superposed loads.

Figure 216 shows the uncommon shape given to some pistols marked LE PAGE MOUTIER PARIS. Both single-shot and superposed load pistols were made in this streamlined version. Triggers on these Le Page pistols fold with perfect fit into the frames. Their engraving so perfectly matches and blends with surrounding designs that the triggers can hardly be detected when folded. The unusually shaped grips have engraved metal ends that appear to be merely ornaments but which actually are covers for concealed cap boxes. The pistol illustrated with only the right hammer cocked is like the second model Lindsay in operation. Cocking only one hammer at a time was a commendable and safe practice, if one were careful to avoid using the left hammer before the forward charge was out of the barrel.

The Le Page 12-shot pepperbox which is shown in two views, figures 217 and 218, is a most exceptional piece. It not only is a true pepperbox using superposed loads—the only such piece I know of—but it is an example of the highly artistic workmanship of which "Le Page, Arquebusier du Roi", was capable. The beautifully carved stock is of ebony with an unusual metal butt cap that will take a lanyard, or that may be used as a skull cracker. The cylinder is numbered from one to twelve, in gold, with two numbers for each of the six barrels. The pepperbox is double-action with a ring trigger that revolves the cylinder. The center hammer at the top is quite different from the usual Mariette construction. The accessories in the case are complete and include special loading equipment to permit simultaneous loading of six balls as well as six powder charges. And the typical Le Page flask is there, of course.

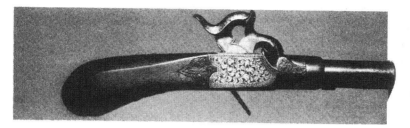

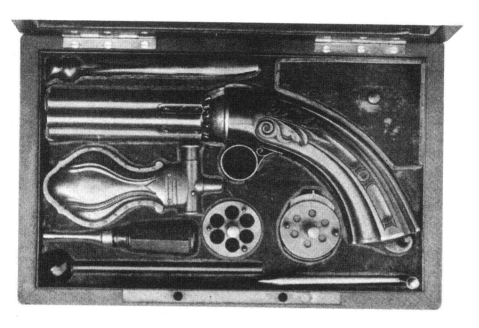

216. Le Page pistol—7¾″ overall/ Frank R. Horner collection.

217. and 218. Le Page pepperbox/ W. Keith Neal collection.

Chapter 10

TURRET AND CHAIN GUNS

NEARLY ALL THE FIREARMS illustrated in this chapter were made well before the American Civil War, but probably none was called a turret gun before the arrival of the Monitor in Hampton Roads in 1862. The revolving superstructure on Ericsson's famous "cheesebox on a raft" is supposed to have given the name turret guns to these odd revolvers. The inventors denominated their creations, "many-chambered-cylinder fire-arms", "many-chambered non-recoil fire arms", "revolving-breech fire-arms", but never used the word turret.

The first pistol illustrated in this chapter is called a wheel pistol and perhaps is not a true turret pistol, but it is a famous oddity.

This percussion cap pistol of unknown origin, figure 219, is 4-shot, about .32 caliber. The wheel which contains the four chambers is in a frame hinged at the bottom and held by screws at the top. The chambers may be loaded at the top without removing the wheel, and the wheel may be rotated by turning a winged screw on the left side, not visible in the illustration. The gun has an iron frame and is very simple in construction. It is not practical—for instance, there is no lock or even catch to insure alignment of the barrel with a chamber—but it is very interesting and most odd in appearance.

Another very odd turret, or wheel, or wheel spoke pistol—we don't know the maker or what he christened it—is in figure 220. We do know the maker of this brass-frame and brass-barrel freak

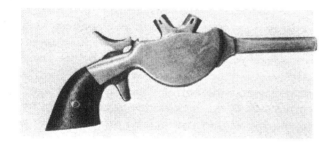

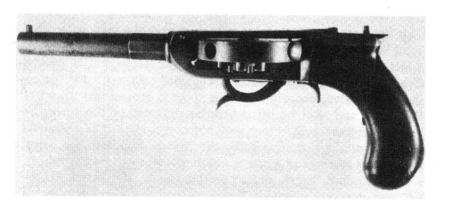

219. Wheel pistol—7½" overall/ Frank R. Horner collection.

220. Wheel spoke pistol/ William M. Locke collection.

221. Allen & Cochran/ Sam E. Smith collection.

went much farther toward achieving complete impracticality than the inventor of the just described wheel pistol. This is true even though this gun does have a catch which will hold the chamber that is under the hammer in line with the barrel. There are six hollow spokes in the revolving turret. These may be loaded with .22 rim-fire cartridges. The cartridges are loaded through an opening in the bottom of the frame. When a cartridge is fired the bullet reaches the barrel only after passing through another chamber. It would be possible to have all six chambers loaded at the same time, but in that event the cartridge under the hammer would have another cartridge directly in front of it, pointing at it, and completely barring passage to the barrel. It is quite impracticable to load more than three chambers at a time. Further, if three chambers be loaded and fired it is necessary to get at least one fired case out of its chamber before firing another cartridge. Otherwise, that fired case will be left directly between the live cartridge and the barrel. There is no extractor. The shell must be pried out. It can be no more than loosened by a rod pushed down the barrel and can not be driven out by a rod inserted in the loading port.

Of the firearms invariably called turret guns by collectors those early ones with horizontal turrets are most esteemed. The most sought of these is one made on the patent granted John W. Cochran, of New York City, April 28, 1837, U. S. patent #188. Illustration 221 is of a 7-shot pistol, serial #106, marked C. B. ALLEN, SPRINGFIELD, MASS., following COCHRAN'S PATENT on the strap above the cylinder. This strap is hinged just ahead of the turret and may be lifted to allow removal of the turret by turning the rear sight, which serves also as a latch. The chambers of the manually turned cylinder are held in line with the barrel by a pin at the end of a spring catch, the pin entering what Mr. Cochran called "catch holes" in the top of the turret. These Cochran guns are unwieldy but seem well made, uncomplicated and not apt to get out of order. The underhammer lock is sturdy and very simple. The danger that caps will fall off and be lost is always present with underhammer guns. Mr. Cochran provided a guard which probably protected the caps as well as possible.

Other guns both long and short made under the Cochran patent may show minor differences in construction. For instance, at least one was 5-shot.

A very rare 5-shot horizontal turret gun is shown in figure 222. The barrel is marked E. H. GRAHAM'S PATENT. Mr. Edmund H. Graham, Hillsborough, New Hampshire, was granted U. S. patent #15734 on September 16, 1856, for an invention designed to prevent accidental multiple explosions of "many-chambered firearms." Isolation of the charge being fired was effected mainly by placing the ball in a chamber at right angles to the chamber containing the powder. The lever on the side rotated the spoke-like cylinder at the same time it cocked the hammer, which is located at the front of the hub.

An interesting horizontal turret pistol invented by Heinrich Genhart, of Belgium, was patented in the United States January 27, 1857, patent # 16447. The example illustrated, figure 223, is 10-shot with the radial chambers each numbered in gold.

On the left side of the frame there is a lever which when pressed down cocks an underhammer and at the same time moves the barrel forward about $\frac{1}{8}''$. The breech end of the barrel will thereby be drawn out of the chamber mouth in which it is retained when the gun is in firing position. In the under face of the turret there are holes, one for each chamber, designed to receive a pin to lock a chamber in line with the barrel. Holding down a small button at the top edge of the frame around the turret will withdraw the pin so the turret may be turned after being freed from the barrel, as just described. When the lever is drawn up, after the cylinder has been manually turned, the barrel re-enters the enlarged mouth of another chamber. The purpose of the close joining was to prevent the escape of gas at the gap between barrel and chamber.

The Genhart gun uses a most unusual cartridge. The guns are scarce but the cartridges are much scarcer. The cartridge is metal and nearly conical. At the powder end the cartridges "are pierced . . . in the line of the longitudinal axis to receive a small metal tube, one end of which extends within the powder, and the other end to about an equal extent outside of the cartridges." This tube was filled with detonating powder. Genhart adapted the Joseph Manton tube lock ignition to a metallic cartridge.

An empty cylinder, or turret, on a Genhart pistol or rifle could be replaced with a loaded spare very quickly with few motions.

Another interesting and rare European turret pistol is shown

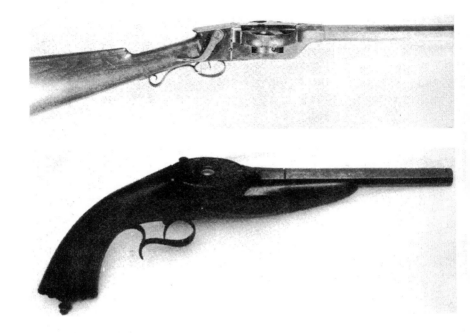

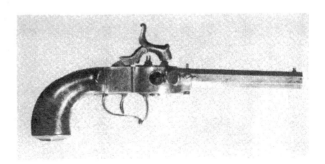

222. Graham rifle/ James E. Serven collection.

223. Genhart pistol—15" overall.

224. Turret pistol/ Henry M. Stewart collection.

in figure 224. This is a 4-shot percussion cap pistol with four nipples on the top face of the horizontal turret. The illustration shows an empty chamber with a hinged gate swung open immediately in front of the chamber mouth. This gate serves to seat the bullet when the chamber is loaded. Cocking the single-action hammer rotates the turret.

There was never marked interest by shooters in any sort of turret guns. The vertical turrets were probably more favorably received than were the horizontal. We find the vertical turret guns in collections in greater numbers and more types.

The best known, in America, of the vertical turret guns is the Porter. A considerable number of Porter rifles exist. Some used standard percussion caps and had nipples in the turrets, but a larger number used a long discontinued type of cap that sent fire to a powder charge directly through a small touch hole in the face of the turret. Though these latter guns did not use the "pill" common at the time we nevertheless refer to these Porters as "pill lock." Mr. John Hintlian let me have an original instruction sheet for "Porter's Cap Box Revolving Rifle" which, because of the large size of the sheet and the small size of the type used in printing it, can not feasibly be reproduced here. This sheet referred to one gun as the "nipple gun" and to the other as the "cap box" gun. Regarding the former, the directions stated "Use Colt's metal lined cap, which fits the nipple well." Regarding the latter there was this, "The cap box contains a spiral spring, which by means of the follower plate, continues to place a cap under the hammer as often as the gun is cocked", and, "The caps should be of a size to fit the groove, so as not to fall in side ways and are placed mouth upwards." Directions as to how to grasp the trigger were explicit, reading, ". . . place three of the fingers into the hand ring, having the fore finger in position to pull the trigger when ready."

Porter pistols, such as the one shown in figure 225, are very scarce. This pistol is constructed much like the rifle in figure 226. The pistol is unmarked; the rifle is marked ADDRESS P. W. PORTER, NEW YORK, PORTER'S PATENT 1851. Both guns are 9-shot and use pill lock ignition. Both have the typical Porter side hammers and automatic primer magazines. The device that rams home the bullets is placed above the barrel on the rifle and below the barrel on the pistol. Movement down and back of the trigger

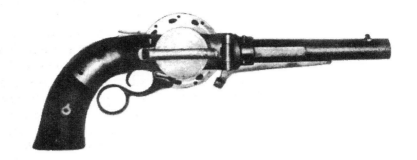

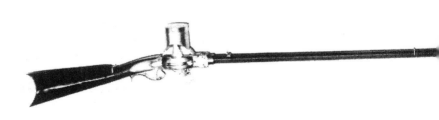

225. Porter revolver—11" overall/ William M. Locke collection.

226. Porter rifle/ James E. Serven collection.

227. Porter rifle/ Smithsonian Institution collection.

guard cocks the hammer and rotates the cylinder, which is easily removed when a catch is released.

A minor fault in vertical turret guns was that the turret obstructed the normal sighting line over the barrel. In some makes front sights were made inordinately high; in at least one make the sights were placed at the right of the barrel so that the gun would have to be held sideways if one were to be able to aim with the sights in the usual upright position. In the Porter guns the sights had abnormally long bases, extending well to the left, so that aiming was alongside rather than over the barrel. More important objections were that all turret guns were unwieldy and expensive. The greatest opposition to the turrets came from the shooter who disliked having bullets in the turret pointing at him. All types of revolvers that did not use modern cartridges with self-contained primers had a propensity to let off all charges at once. Such a multiple discharge was always dangerous.

We know very little about Mr. Porter. There is even disagreement as to his first name. However, Mr. Porter, who stated he lived in Memphis, Tennessee, obtained U. S. patent #8,210 on July 8, 1851, and the patent papers indicate his given name was Parry. Mr. Porter's patent was for a highly impractical gun potentially even more dangerous than the manufactured article. The original idea was to have a magazine, containing powder, balls, and caps, fastened over the turret so that movement of a lever would not only cock the hammer and rotate the turret—it would also load the chambers. The lever movement would also place a cap on a nipple in the turret, as well as strip off a previously detonated cap. The magazine was intended to contain enough powder for thirty shots. A spark might reach and explode that powder at the first shot.

Perhaps the only Porter rifle made with the "cylindrical vessel", as Mr. Porter called it, which contained powder, balls, and percussion caps in separate compartments, is shown in figure 227.

According to Van Rensselaer, Porter rifles were manufactured in Taunton, Massachusetts by George Foster, without the outlandish magazine, of course.

Another vertical turret pistol was patented November 7, 1854, by Wendell Wright of New York City, U. S. patent #11,917. This extremely rare piece is illustrated in figure 228. The gun is 8-shot, about .36 caliber, and uses what the inventor called "detonating pills" for ignition. These pills are contained in a boss on the side of the turret and are automatically fed one at a time to the touch holes when the turret is revolved. There are two triggers. To fire the gun as a repeating pistol, the curved "cocking trigger" under the turret is drawn back after the straight trigger (called the "thumb trigger" and seen back of the hammer) is pressed against the stock. The curved trigger rotates the cylinder, cocks the hammer, and presses a stop in a chamber mouth to index the cylinder. The straight trigger first permits movement of the curved trigger so the latter may withdraw the cylinder stop and then proceed with its other just described duties. Finally, the thumb trigger if pressed down at a time the curved trigger is fully retracted, will release the hammer.

Mr. Wright had several novel ideas. One was a flexible pin on the end of the hammer, secured by india-rubber, designed to compensate for "any moderate aberration in the descent of the hammer" and so prevent misfires.

Illustration 229 shows a double-action Noel pistol of about 1860 that is probably the most frequently found of the European turret pistols. The example shown is marked J. F. GOUDRY PARIS and SYSTEME A NOEL. Pulling the folding trigger raises and drops a side hammer and also revolves the 10-shot turret. By raising a large gate on the left this turret may be quickly withdrawn for reloading or for replacement with another already loaded turret. There is an interesting safety device which can be so placed as to prevent the long hammer nose entering the vent which leads to the powder chamber. When the trigger is pulled the safety automatically drops away and lets the hammer nose detonate the fulminate.

Two other unmarked, probably European, pistols are shown in figures 230 and 231. One has a large hammer with a long nose to reach the fulminate priming. This is shown cocked for use as single-action, but it may be fired double-action. Its vertical turret, which instead of being solid has a round opening in the center, has six .42 caliber chambers and may be removed when the hinged plate on the right side is opened. The sights have very peculiar features. The front sight is, in shooters' terminology, at three o'clock on the barrel. The rear sight is the kerf in the head of the screw which may be said to be hanging on the edge of the hinged plate at nine o'clock. Part of the screw head is cut away

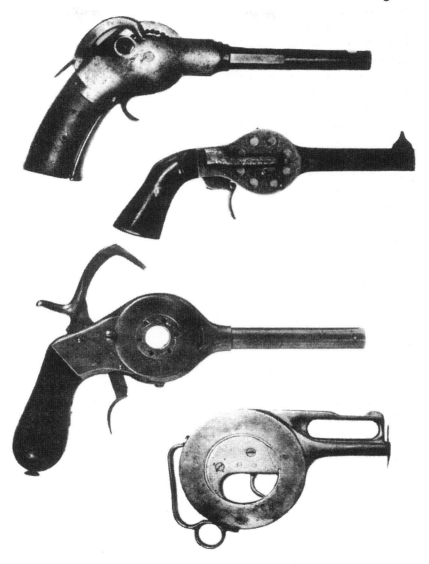

228. Wright revolver—10″ overall/ William M. Locke collection.

229. French turret revolver.

230. Turret revolver/ Frank R. Horner collection.

231. 18-shot revolver/ Dr. W. R. Funderburg collection.

close to the shank, so the plate may be swung free when the screw is sufficiently turned. The other pistol, figure 231, is heavy and unhandy. Its turret is a ring-like disc with eighteen chambers, by no means easy to remove for reloading. Modern small caliber cartridges are discharged by a firing pin drawn back and released when the trigger is pulled. Trigger pull also rotates the circular magazine. The superstructure built on the barrel serves no purpose other than to hold the sights.

The various Protector pistols are also turret pistols. They were described in the chapter on Squeezers and Knuckledusters.

The repeating pistols that are fitted with revolving chains as magazines are odder and scarcer than those fitted with revolving turrets.

An American 20-shot chain pistol patented January 23, 1866, by Harry S. Josselyn, Roxbury, Massachusetts, U. S. patent #52,248, is shown in figure 232. The endless steel chain, with a chamber for a .22 rim-fire cartridge in each link, turns around a sprocket wheel having six teeth. Cocking the hammer rotates the sprocket wheel by means of a pawl. A spring-latch attached to the hammer holds each cartridge as it comes around in line with the barrel, when the trigger is pulled.

An almost identical system of endless chain and sprocket wheel was used in an earlier British invention, patented by Thomas Treeby, London, British patent #1552 of the year 1855.

As in the Josselyn, the chain, or endless belt of chambers on the Treeby is rotated by the cocking of the hammer. The lower end of the chain on the Josselyn gun swings freely, there being only one sprocket wheel. On the Treeby gun illustrated, figure 233, uncontrolled swinging is prevented by use of a second sprocket wheel placed at the bottom of the loop and held by straps running down from the frame. This feature, the second sprocket, was not included in Mr. Treeby's 1855 patent, but it was patented by him as an improvement in his patent #1306 in the year 1858.

A more important feature of the Treeby is the method of getting a gas-tight joint between barrel and chamber. A tight joint is made by moving the barrel back into locked connection with a chamber mouth. The Genhart turret pistol described earlier in this chapter uses the same idea of backward movement of the barrel for obturation. In the Genhart the barrel simply

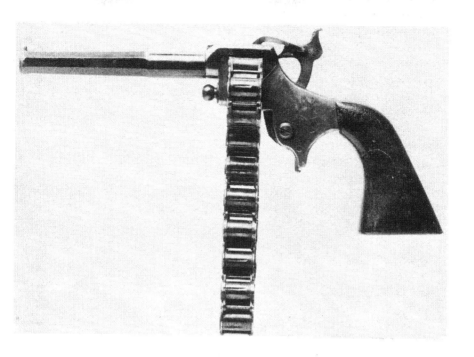

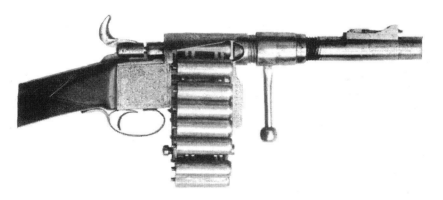

232. Josselyn pistol/ Smithsonian Institution collection.

233. Treeby rifle/ Photograph courtesy Harold G. Young.

slides back when a lever is raised. In the Treeby the turning of a bolt handle attached to a sleeve causes forward or backward movement of the barrel.

Only about a quarter turn of the bolt handle is required to free the barrel from a chamber mouth so the chain may revolve. To facilitate firm closing of the joint there is a handhold about the length of and just in back of the bolt handle.

The gun in the illustration has a chain with fourteen chambers. A Treeby gun demonstrated before instructors of musketry at Hythe was fitted with a chain having thirty chambers. It was fired from the shoulder, with a rest for the barrel, and discharged its thirty shots in less than a minute. The gun was designed for military use as a defensive weapon. It was accurate and probably capable of the best sustained rapid fire of any gun of the time, but it did not fire a heavy charge and was not considered adequate for use by the armed services.

The best known of the endless chain guns is a French product, the Guýcot. The gun is usually referred to as the "forty shot belt pistol." It happens I have never seen one known to be forty shot, but I have had pistols in 25-shot and 32-shot, and rifles in 80-shot and 100-shot. Figure 234 shows a 25-shot pistol and figure 235 shows part of the mechanism of a 100-shot rifle. In the latter illustration perhaps 25 of the cartridge carrying cups are discernible. The other 75 are inside the stock. The endless chain, or belt, that carries the cups extends all the way to the butt plate.

Once the gun is loaded it may be fired as fast as the trigger can be pulled. As the trigger is pulled, the belt is revolved until a chamber faces the barrel. At the same time a long firing pin is retracted. Then an inner barrel is drawn back through the heavy outer barrel until it covers the bullet end of the cartridge. When the long drag on the trigger ends, the final pressure releases the needle-like firing pin, which drives through the small opening in the base of the cup-like container to detonate the cartridge primer.

The engagement of barrel breech and chamber mouth at the moment of firing is again by drawing back the barrel, as in the Treeby and in the Genhart. I do not recall any other guns that attempt to get tight joints by pulling back the barrel to the chamber mouth. Pressing a chamber mouth forward against a

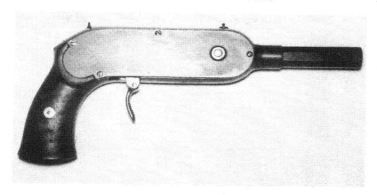

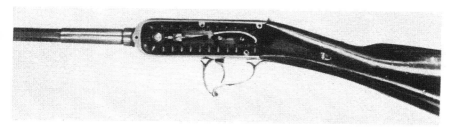

234. 25-shot chain pistol/ Eddie Reider collection.

235. 100-shot chain rifle.

236. Enouy's revolver/ Photograph courtesy Sam E. Smith.

barrel breech is a better known method. That was done in the flintlock Collier revolvers, in the percussion cap Savage revolvers, and in other guns.

It should be explained that there is a button on the left of the frame which is kept down at the bottom of a groove when the gun is to be fired. If the button is pressed up when the trigger is not drawn back the gun is completely locked and the belt will not revolve.

Reloading one of these guns is a problem that requires a neat maneuver to solve. Cartridges are placed in the cups of the belt carrier one at a time through a slot on top of the frame. After one cartridge is inserted in a cup it is necessary to pull the trigger to revolve the carrier so another cup may be loaded. In order to prevent the discharge of the first cartridge after about a dozen cartridges are loaded, the locking button just referred to is raised after the trigger has been drawn partly back, with the result the firing pin is kept back but the belt moves when the trigger is pulled.

This chapter seems the proper place for the 42-shot "Ferris Wheel" pistol shown in figure 236, although the revolving framework which holds the "compound magazine", as its inventor called it, can hardly be called a chain. The inventor was Joseph Enouy, who obtained British patent #1359 of the year 1855. The gun is a percussion cap double-action revolver of the transition type which used the top hammer construction of the earlier English pepperboxes. It is equipped with a revolving framework having an axle fastened to the grip and to the barrel as the illustration shows. There are seven spokes to the wheel, and at the outer end of each spoke is a cylinder with six chambers. When one cylinder is empty the framework is turned so a loaded cylinder may be locked in position for firing.

Chapter 11

MISCELLANEOUS

Here we find outstanding examples of the wise and the foolish, and also, on unsure footing, a few firearms that some collectors will deny recognition as curiosa.

Because "A Hair perhaps divides the False and True" it is impossible that any two collectors will always agree in separating the unconventional from the established order.

We may say a gun to be classed as curiosa must have some bizarre feature that tends to astonish the student—but just what is a bizarre feature? We may say an oddity will always provoke either a sympathetic smile or a derisive laugh—but, are collectors' risibilities all triggered alike? Let him first square the circle, who would define "oddity."

There are many rare and odd guns with remarkable ignition systems or repeating mechanisms—Forsyths, Fergusons, Colliers —that are excluded here. This is not a history of firearms.

Arbitrarily excluded are all firearms incapable of shooting. (A gun intended only for blank cartridges but which can fire a bullet is not necessarily excluded.) I was offered for illustration as an oddity a magnificent tinderlighter made by Boutet. It looked like a flint pistol, but when the trigger was pulled the barrel flew open and there was a lighted candle. That lighter does not shoot, and so is not illustrated here, but if any collector of firearms does not want it in his collection he is daft. Whether he collects oddities, lowly pepperboxes, or important Brescian snaphaunces.

I respectfully suggest to the reader that the more he limits his collection the more he limits interest in it.

There are many special purpose weapons worthy of consideration by the collector, though omitted from this book—punt guns, harpoon guns, rescue guns used by fire departments and coastguardmen to throw lines, marking guns used by police and automobile men to determine efficiency of drivers and brakes. And if a collector likes to include a cigar cutter shaped like a pistol— I see no reason why he should not.

Some guns reveal at a glance their freakishness; others hide their peculiarities from all but the student. An extreme example of each type is shown in figures 237 and 238.

Illustration 237 is a reproduction of the frontispiece from the August, 1912, issue of *Magazine of Antique Firearms*. The caption for the frontispiece reads, "C. Bechtler's Double Ender Pistol. A Southern made pistol of great rarity. Fisher collection." An accompanying article by Dr. A. L. Fisher explains that the mainspring is the trigger guard and that this mainspring may be released by either trigger. Dr. Fisher notes that as the two hammers can not both be cocked at the same time, simultaneous murder and suicide can not be accomplished! The gun is sometimes known as the "Fore and Aft" and is assumed to have been made by Christopher Bechtler. Mr. Bechtler was a German gunsmith who settled in Rutherford, North Carolina, in 1829. Certainly a collector may need a second look to be sure his eyes have not deceived him, but not to decide that this is truly an oddity.

A gun just like the one in illustration 238 is to be found in many collections. It is the excellent but much misunderstood percussion cap rifle invented by Lieutenant-Colonel J. Durrell Greene, U. S. Army, and patented November 17, 1857, U. S. patent #18,634. It has several unusual features. It is the first bolt-action rifle adopted by the U. S. Army. (Considerable numbers of Greene rifles, of which 900 or more were purchased by the U. S. Army, saw service in the Civil War.) It is the first underhammer rifle adopted by the U. S. Army. (If any one say at this point that these facts do not make the gun an oddity, I fully agree.) It is the only oval-bored rifle adopted by the U. S. Army. Here is where a couple of misunderstandings come in. First, any one who takes the bolt out of a Greene rifle and looks through the barrel will see a smooth bore with no lands or grooves. Only if he be familiar with the Lancaster system of barrel boring can he

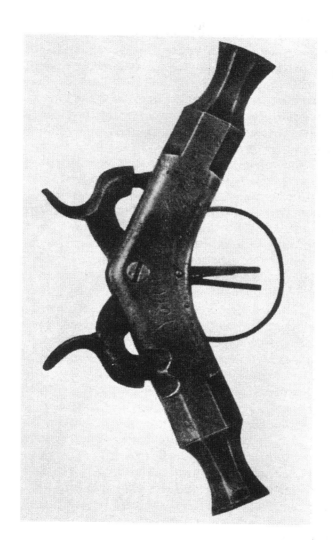

237. Bechtler Double-Ender pistol/ Photograph courtesy Robert Abels.

understand why the Greene is called a rifle. Second, many collectors incorrectly think an oval-bored barrel requires a bullet with elliptical cross-section. It may be well to quote here from an 1864 U. S. Ordnance report on the Greene—". . . the bore is elliptical in shape, and the rotary motion is imparted to the bullet by giving the longest diameter of the ellipse a turn of three-fourths in the length of the barrel. The oval form is too slight a variation from a perfect cylinder to be perceptible to the eye, and the appearance of the barrel, on looking through, is precisely like that of a smoothbore musket. But by placing one of the bullets (*which are cast round, and assume the elliptical shape on entering the barrel*) into the muzzle, and looking through from the breech, a slight crescent of light will be perceived on each side of it." The italicizing of the parenthetical quotation is mine.

I do not press the argument that the gun is an oddity simply because it is a rifle though it looks like a smoothbore. Oval boring was in use in England thirty years before our Civil War, and being tried out in this country as something new forty years after. About the turn of the century this system of oval-bore rifling was submitted by some one, as a new invention, to the Ordnance Department, and tests were made in Krags and experimental Springfields. In respect of flatter trajectory, increased initial accuracy, sustained accuracy, ease of cleaning and decreased bore wear, the oval-bore rifling apparently had the edge over conventional rifling. However, in one match, one group of men made a slightly better score with a regular service rifle than another group made with a rifle with oval bore.

The Greene has another unusual feature. This one is odd to the extent of being unique. It completely reverses accepted practice, but it is evident only to the student. The Greene fires a combustible paper cartridge that contains its bullet in its base, back of its powder charge. The cartridge is capable of shooting a bullet from the previously fired cartridge, but never its own bullet.

Starting with an empty rifle, loading was as follows. A safety button on the breech tang, which locked the bolt and prevented firing unless the bolt were home, was pressed down, permitting the bolt handle to be turned up and the bolt drawn back. With the bolt back, a hollow-base expanding bullet was dropped in the receiver. The bolt was moved forward to its original closed position but the bolt handle was not then turned down. Forward

238. and 239. Greene rifle/ Harold G. Young collection.

pressure was continued on the bolt handle, and an auxiliary rod, or inner bolt, moved ahead to seat the bullet. This position is shown in figure 238. Again the bolt was drawn fully back, and, after a cartridge was placed in the receiver, was moved forward sufficiently to push the cartridge into the chamber. The bolt handle was turned down, the ring hammer was cocked by a pull with the index finger, the nipple was capped, and the gun was ready to fire when the trigger was pulled. Figure 239 shows this position. On pulling the trigger the forward bullet left the gun, but the bullet at the base of the just discharged cartridge had not moved, and it had served as a very efficient gas check. It was now ready to be pushed forward and fired by the next cartridge.

It is my belief that much more than half the Greene rifles in collections have the concentric inner bolt frozen tight so the bolt handle cannot assume the position shown in figure 238. Careful application of heat will usually free the parts without difficulty.

Placing the primer ahead of the powder in a cartridge hardly seems as absurd as placing the bullet behind the powder, as in the just described Greene rifle, but to me a gun that uses such a cartridge gets the nod as an oddity.

The Greene rifle, with the bullet back of the powder, was of very little influence in the outcome of our Civil War. Its cartridge did create a little excitement among men who wrongly assumed the foremost end was the bullet end, and who thought the big end of the bullet, not the point, was the striking end. From there they went completely off the rails, reaching the conclusion the hollow end of the bullet contained poison and was placed foremost so the poison would be spread around in the wound.

On the other hand the Dreyse needle gun, with its primer ahead of the powder, probably influenced the course of world events more than any other firearm in history—after the Forsyth invention, that is. It has been called "the great granddaddy of all bolt action rifles . . . the magic wand with which the various Germanic states were united to form Germany under the Hohenzollern dynasty."* Its importance is undeniable, but we are concerned here with needle guns only from the standpoint of oddity.

The German needle gun employs a long needle-like firing pin which is driven through the center of the base of a combustible cartridge and on through the powder to detonate a primer resting

* Article by Edward D. Crabb in the American Rifleman, February, 1941.

at the base of the bullet. The bullet serves as an anvil. The firing pin was surrounded by burning powder when the fulminate priming was detonated and so its life was shortened. The theoretical advantage in igniting the powder at the base of the bullet was that the burning of the powder from front to rear resulted in higher bullet velocity.

Illustration 240 is of a Dreyse military rifle of 1848. This is a true needle gun. There exist many guns that use needle-like firing pins—the most remarkable probably being the Pauly breechloader which was invented in 1812 and used a center-fire self-contained cartridge—but these guns, which did not use the primer-ahead-of-the-powder cartridges, are here considered neither needle guns nor oddities.

The gun shown is the first type of military breechloader. The bolt handle works the same as in modern bolt-action guns, in that it is raised and pulled back, and then, after a cartridge is dropped in the receiver, pressed forward and down—but this action on the Dreyse does not complete preparation for firing. On the gun shown it is necessary to draw back a thumb piece before opening the bolt, and to push back this piece after closing the bolt.

The long German needle guns, whether military or sporting, muzzle-loading or breech-loading, were not odd in appearance. The rare needle-fire revolvers are quite odd in appearance. Their shape was peculiar because room had to be provided back of the cylinder for a mechanism that would drive the needle deep in the chamber and instantly withdraw it after detonating the fulminate. The only true needle-fire revolvers I know of were made by Dreyse. Two types of these rare guns are shown together, figure 241. The larger is 8-shot of about .45 caliber, the smaller is 6-shot of slightly smaller caliber. The long lever, partly covered with wood, on the larger revolver, serves to cock the gun, also to revolve and lock the cylinder. This lever must be held close against the grip when the trigger is pulled. The smaller revolver is conventionally double-action in that both the turning of the cylinder and the firing of the cartridge require no more than a pull of the trigger.

To go back to the guns that shoot both ways—figure 242 illustrates a modern version of the Double Ender. Like Bechtler's Double Ender, this can not fire in both directions simultaneously, but it has two steel barrels screwed on a center portion and

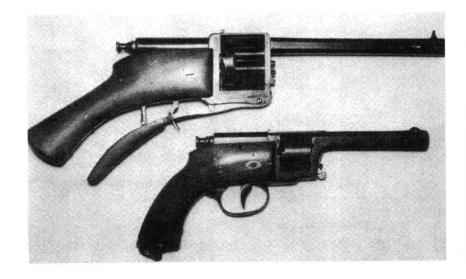

240. Dreyse rifle.

241. Two Dreyse revolvers—top 16½" overall/ Frank R. Horner collection.

pointing in opposite directions. The gun is intended for use with rather large gas cartridges. The gun is grasped in the center and fired by pulling back a spring-controlled plunger and then releasing it. After one barrel is fired the piece may be quickly turned and the other barrel fired.

There was at least one gun that actually did shoot both ways at once. It had a double length barrel, with one end rifled and the other smooth. A brass cartridge had powder in the middle, a solid projectile at one end, and very fine shot at the other. On firing, the projectile went one way out the rifled end and the charge of shot went the other way out the smooth end. The idea was to reduce recoil. The gun was tried out in airplanes in World War I.

The rare cartridge derringer patented June 21, 1864 by Samuel M. Perry, has a barrel that can be loaded at either end with a .41 rim-fire cartridge. The inventor most definitely did not intend that the barrel have loaded shells in both ends at the same time, but he did expect that often when a loaded shell in one end was fired there would be an empty, just fired, shell in the other end. In fact, the object of the invention was to have ". . . the spent cartridge-shell . . . expelled from the chamber of the barrel by the explosion of the succeeding cartridge."

It happened that two of these rare pistols were simultaneously made available to me for study. Figure 243 shows one gun with the barrel swung out; figure 244 shows the other gun with the barrel closed. These may be the only "Double Headers" remaining in existence. Where they were made is unknown.

The first illustration shows the barrel ready for loading. The barrel has both ends chambered and recessed for cartridge rims, and may be turned through 180°. When lined up with the frame and in firing position the barrel is held by a spring catch.

The inventor properly claimed the pistol could be fired more rapidly than any other derringer because its operation required fewer motions. After the first shot the operation required to get another loaded cartridge under the hammer consisted simply in loading a cartridge at the muzzle and turning the barrel end for end. With other single-shot cartridge derringers it was necessary to open the breech, eject the empty shell, reload, and close the breech—three or four motions, instead of two.

The spent case of the first cartridge was expelled from the

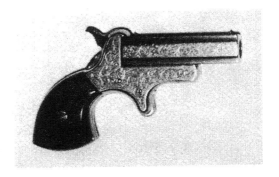

242. Gas pistol/ H. Gordon Frost collection.

243. Double Header/ Paul S. Foster collection.

244. Double Header/ William M. Locke collection.

muzzle by the second discharge, supposedly "in advance of the ball."

The two guns illustrated are identically marked DOUBLE HEADER E. S. RENWICK MANUF'R NEW-YORK PAT. JUNE 21, 1864. E. S. Renwick was the assignee of the two patents, numbers 43,259 and 43,260, granted Samuel M. Perry, June 21, 1864. Another patent, #102,429, also assigned to Renwick, was applied for by Samuel M. Perry and Emerson Goddard in 1867 but not granted until April 26, 1870. This patent covered an improved catch for "holding the movable barrel in the position for firing." On the front page of the November 18, 1868, *Scientific American* is an article headed "Patent Copper Cartridge Revolving Derringer", and an illustration captioned "The Perry and Goddard, 'Double Header', or 'Perpetual Revolver'." The article suggested that anyone interested in "the purchase of the entire right or for an exclusive license to manufacture under the patents" should address E. S. Renwick, 34 Beach St., New York City. An 1869 New York City directory lists Edward S. Renwick as a Solicitor of Patents with an office at 34 Beach Street.

The pistol illustrated in the 1868 *Scientific American* had the 1870 patent improvement. It would seem that only guns with this improvement should rightfully be called Perry and Goddard. Goddard was concerned as a patentee only with the improved catch. Whether or not any derringers were made for sale under the 1870 patent, I do not know. Neither of the two derringers illustrated here has the movable button, under the frame, which is the outward evidence of the improved catch.

If any one ever fired a Double Header with loaded cartridges at both ends of the barrel the results have not been recorded.

Of the oddities among military weapons none has received more publicity than the Puckle gun. Illustration 245 is a reproduction of the British patent granted in 1718 to James Puckle of London, for what Mr. Puckle described as ". . . a Portable Gun or Machine (by me lately Invented) called a DEFENCE . . ."

The Puckle invention was probably the first crank-operated machine gun. It embodied several elements that closely resemble construction features of Gatling, Hotchkiss and other manually-operated machine guns. The Puckle gun has been many times mentioned in connection with modern machine guns, and the Puckle patent many times referred to in actions at law. Probably

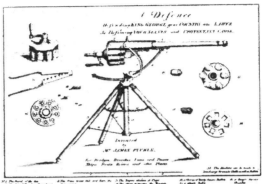

245. British patent drawing—Puckle gun.

no one who has commented on the Puckle gun, whether in the courts of law or in a serious treatise on the development of machine guns, has been able to refrain from telling about the square bullets. So here it is, once more. Illustrated directly under the muzzle of the gun are two "plates of chambers." The lower is described in the patent as "16. The plate of the Chambers of the Gun for a Ship shooting Square Bullets against Turks." The upper is described as "17. For Round Bullets against Christians."

It is doubtful that any of the Puckle guns that may have been actually produced ever saw service. A contemporaneous poet, commenting on "Puckle's Machine Company", wrote

"Fear not, my friends, this terrible machine.
They're only wounded who have shares therein."

Cavities have been cut in gun stocks to hold patch boxes, as in Kentucky rifles, to contain repeating mechanisms, as in Spencer rifles, and for a hundred other purposes. Stocks have had wood cut away to provide space for extra parts, extra cartridges, tools, telescopes, knives, even music boxes. Of the many guns with stocks hollowed out two only will be shown here as oddities. Both guns are very rare American martial arms, highly prized by collectors. Illustration 246 is of a Colt with a canteen stock; illustrations 247 and 248 are of a coffee mill Sharps.

The Colt is an Old Model Navy Pistol fitted with a canteen shoulderstock patented by Samuel Colt, January 18, 1859, patents numbers 22,626 and 22,627. The first of these patents dealt with the method of ". . . coupling the removable stock to pistols in forming the carbine-pistol attachment . . ." The second patent claimed "So constructing the stock of a gun that it shall constitute a canteen . . ." The hollow interior of the stock is fitted with a metal-lined ". . . reservoir having a suitable opening and stopper . . ."

Illustration 247 shows a vertical breech Sharps carbine, fitted with a coffee mill. The Government bought about 80,000 Sharps percussion cap carbines for use in the American Civil War, and planned to have each cavalry company that was outfitted with the Sharps supplied with one gun having a coffee mill in the butt. The coffee beans were poured in the mill through an opening underneath the stock. The ground coffee came out on the other side of the butt from the crank, through the small curved opening in the plate shown in figure 248.

246. Canteen Stock Colt/ William M. Locke collection.

247. and 248. Coffee mill Sharps/ John K. Watson collection.

The peculiar pistol shown in illustrations 249 and 250 is stamped HAND FIRING MECHANISM MK-2. It was used by specially trained personnel in World War II and was named a "fist gun" in the patent #2,423,448, granted Stanley M. Haight, United States Navy, July 8, 1947. The patent application was filed February 29, 1944.

One view shows the fist gun on the back of a glove, in firing position, with "a trigger projecting from the firearm closely adjacent and forward of (the) muzzle." The other view shows the gun removed from the glove and with the barrel swung up for loading. The gun is a single-shot pistol, using a .38 S & W cartridge. As soon as this pistol is loaded and the barrel pushed down to the firing position, pressure on the knob alongside the barrel muzzle will discharge the cartridge. As the patent states, "When the fist is doubled up, the trigger is exposed for contact and the fingers are removed from the line of fire", and "a lethal charge can be discharged into an adversary by pressing or striking the weapon against him." A slide safety is provided so the gun will not be fired accidentally. The pistol shown is an improvement on the original Haight patent in that it does not require a separate device to cock the striker.

Another special gun of World War II is shown in 251. This is usually called the .45 Underground Pistol, getting its name from the fact it was especially designed for supply to our "underground allies." The gun is an unprepossessing low-cost stamped-metal product of which a million or more were secretly made and dropped behind enemy lines. Despite its crude appearance, the gun is fully able to handle its powerful .45 auto cartridge. The pistol is single-shot, of course, with no provision for mechanical extraction of a fired case. The empty could be pushed out with anything suitable that was handy—a pencil would do. The pistol's hollow grip would hold extra cartridges.

To load the gun, the hammer is first drawn back and turned. Then a sliding breech plate is raised, a cartridge inserted in the barrel, the breech plate pressed down, and the hammer turned back until its long firing pin will enter a hole in the top of the breech plate. The gun is now ready for firing.

In the package with each gun dropped there was ammunition and also a sign language instruction sheet explaining the loading and operation.

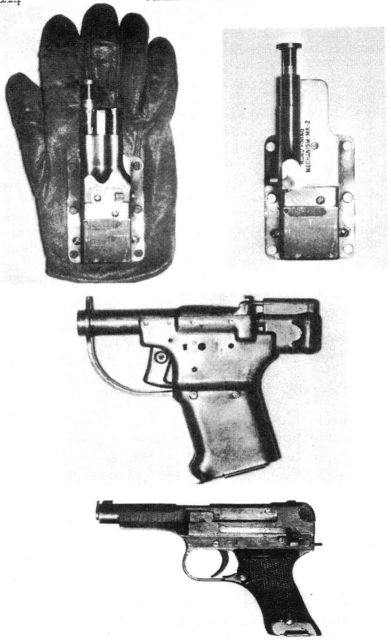

249. and 250. Fist pistol/ Martin B. Retting collection.
251. .45 underground pistol/ Governor Gordon Persons collection.
252. Japanese autoloading pistol/ Dr. W. R. Funderburg collection.

The guns were of much value to irregulars in enabling them to obtain the better weapons carried by an isolated enemy regular, such as a sentry.

The Japanese autoloading pistol shown in figure 252 may be fired by pressing on a long lever in the side of the frame, without touching the trigger. The U. S. forces issued a bulletin in World War II to warn personnel of the possible danger that these guns might be fired intentionally by an enemy without his touching the trigger, or unintentionally by any one who examined the gun without being familiar with its operation.

The pistol is commonly called the Japanese Suicide Automatic. The story back of the name is reasonable to those who know that the Japanese who commits suicide will make the momentous act as impressive and ceremonious as possible, but it is given here without assurance of its truth. Supposedly, a Japanese officer having one of these guns would use it for suicide at the moment he presented it to his captor. The gun would be held in the acceptably correct manner for surrendering it, butt foremost with the barrel pointing toward the abdomen and the fingers around the barrel. At the final instant of surrender the thumb would be pressed on the tip of the long lever which is visible in the photograph just above the trigger.

A misfire due to a fault in a fresh modern cartridge is today almost unknown. Misfires in muzzle-loading weapons, particularly flintlocks, were commonplace.

A misfire in a flintlock sometimes resulted from a worn, or broken, or badly set flint—though it could result from fouling, careless priming, weak springs, inferior steel, or just bad weather. Illustration 253 shows a Tower belt pistol with a lock designed to get a useless flint quickly replaced by means of a cock with a double pair of jaws, facing in opposite directions. The length of time a flint gun was out of action while a spare flint was screwed in position in the usual way, could be greatly reduced by use of this lock. Getting a new flint in position required only swinging the double head around after loosening a wing nut.

Sir Howard Douglas submitted the idea of this lock, presumably his invention, to the British Army authorities in 1817. It was apparently thoroughly tested, but was considered to be clumsy and troublesome. The lock had some success in its use on cannon of the British Navy, but none in use on pistols, rifles or muskets.

An old Bannerman catalogue shows another pistol fitted with a Douglas lock, and examples of muskets and rifles so equipped are in the Tower of London.

The idea of the Douglas lock was to have a spare flint ready to be put in use with the least possible delay. Having a complete extra lock available was an idea that found favor even before the days of flintlocks. Illustration 254 is of a Brescian matchlock sporting gun with two serpentines which operate separately with different triggers. One trigger is the early form of long lever, and the serpentine it actuates is the slow moving type. The other trigger is a button, and the serpentine it releases is one that flies down suddenly. The gun is single-shot and has but one pan. The two serpentines have small split ends, too small to grip match cord of normal size. Bits of burning tinder, ignited from a separate match, were used in such serpentines. Some students prefer to call such guns "tinder lock", rather than "matchlock".

Sometimes two different types of ignition were made available. Figure 255 is of a plain military piece provided with both a wheel lock and a matchlock. The illustration shows the doghead in position so that if the wheel were spanned, and if pyrites were in place in the jaws of the doghead, pressure on the trigger would spin the wheel and send sparks into the pan. The ignition by means of a burning match is in reserve. To use that, the doghead would be pulled back so it would not interfere with the serpentine. Trigger pressure would guide the serpentine to the pan when the wheel lock was not in use. This serpentine is of the usual size to hold match cord.

Some guns were made which fired two locks at the same time. This double ignition, as a safety measure in an emergency, is certainly more valuable than a reserve lock if there will be no time to fire the second lock. A flint pistol by Barbar, London, which has two hammers that go down together when the trigger is pulled, is shown in figure 256. In addition to the two hammers there are of course two frizzens and two pans with vents both leading to the one powder charge.

A single-shot dagger pistol which uses percussion cap double ignition is shown in two views, figures 257 and 258. This is a French piece, marked CORREVON A YVERDON. There are two nipples that lead to the powder chamber. The hammer is bifurcated and has two hammer noses. When the trigger is pulled two caps

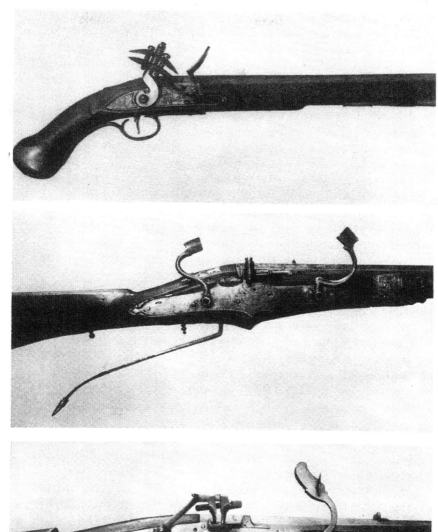

253. Douglas pistol—19″ overall.
254. Brescian matchlock.
255. Matchlock-wheel lock.

are detonated simultaneously.

The unusually long dagger, when held under the stock, may be released by pressing a button under the grip. It will then be thrust out and locked in place by a heavy spring under the barrel.

The dagger pistol has one hammer with two noses that simultaneously hit two nipples. The pistol in illustration 259 has one hammer with only one nose, but it too hits two nipples simultaneously, and in this case the vents lead to two over-and-under barrels. If the objective is to assure a discharge at the first trigger pull, this system seems most likely to succeed. The probability that of two barrels, each with one nipple, one will fire, is greater than that one barrel will fire if equipped with two nipples. The gun is very slim, and it has British proof marks, though no maker's name.

This use of two caps to be detonated simultaneously to discharge two barrels at the same time is much less frequently encountered than the use of a single cap to discharge several barrels at once, or of a single flintlock to accomplish the same result. Long guns with multiple barrels all fired at once by one lock have been popular for wildfowl shooting since the first ones, flintlock and called volley guns, were made by Henry Nock. Some of the trap guns mentioned in Chapter VI are of this multiple explosion type.

Of the guns with multiple barrels that fire simultaneously one eagerly sought by collectors is the Duckfoot or Mob Pistol. An example made by Twigg, London, circa 1780, is shown in figure 260. The bullets from the four barrels are discharged together but they go in different directions within a sector of a circle. The weapon was an effective deterrent to holdup men at close quarters and seems to have been developed for bank runners. It is reputed to have become popular with prison guards and tough sea captains. Any member of a mob was given pause by the knowledge he was jeopardizing his fellows if he rushed a man who pointed one of these splay-barrelled pistols in his direction.

Another pistol with four barrels that fire together is in figure 261. This piece made by J. Hunt, London, is noticeably different from the Twigg in that its barrels are designed to place four bullets in a small group, rather than spread them.

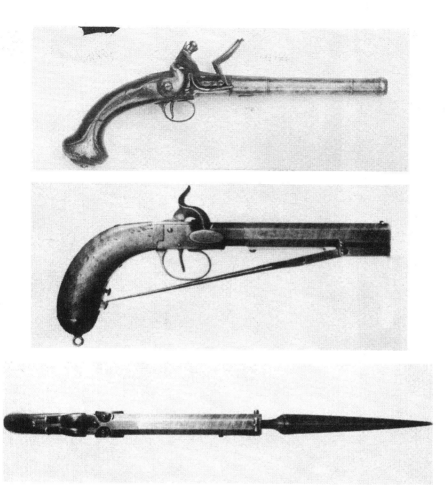

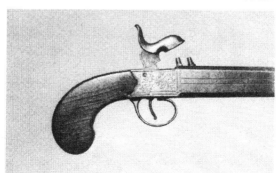

256. Barbar pistol—13" overall/ Joseph Kindig, Jr. collection.
257. and 258. Correvon pistol.
259. Two-barrel pistol/ Frank R. Horner collection.

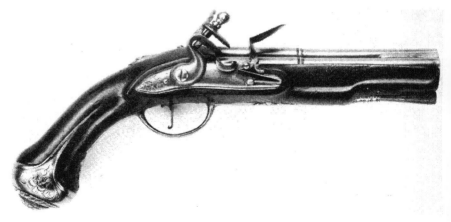

260. Duckfoot pistol.

261. Hunt pistol/ Joseph Kindig, Jr. collection.

262. Flint pepperbox/ William M. Locke collection.

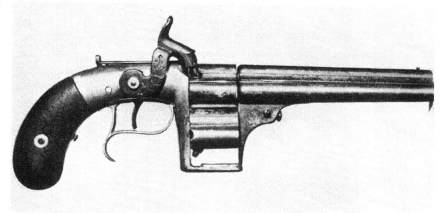

263. Double pepperbox/ Governor Gordon Persons collection.

264. Three-barrel pistol/ Sam E. Smith collection.

265. Durs Egg pistol.

A six-barrel pistol, illustrated in figure 262, has all its barrels fired by a single pull of the trigger. The discharges are not exactly simultaneous though they must sound as an uninterrupted roar. They might properly be called momentaneous, as they begin and terminate in an instant. Each barrel, after the first, is fired by ignition from the preceding charge. This is managed by having the barrel bores progressively decreased in length with vents connecting the barrels so fire will go from the first barrel to ignite powder in the chamber of the second barrel, and so on.

In illustration 263 is a most curious cartridge gun with eight barrels. The eight barrels are arranged in two groups of four barrels each, and the eight charges may be fired all at once or four at a time. This very attractive piece is Italian and has several unusual features. It is marked MITRAGLIERA PRIVILEGIATA SISTEMA MEROLLA GIOVANNI. The barrels in each group diverge both vertically and horizontally, so a burst of shots spreads both sideways and up and down. There are two hammers, each striking two firing pins, with each firing pin striking two cartridge heads. By means of a clip that folds over the cartridge heads, eight cartridges may be loaded in one movement when the barrels are tipped down. Four vertical slots in the back of the clip permit each firing pin to strike one top cartridge and also the cartridge immediately below at the same instant. The trigger is a button under the barrel which moves forward when a hammer is cocked, and which fires by a squeeze of the finger tip. A squeeze on the trigger fires eight cartridges if both hammers are cocked; it fires four if the left hammer only is cocked.

The most fantastic of the guns that fire more than one shot at a time is the nine-chamber, three-barrel revolver in illustration 264 which fires three shots at a time. This is marked on the left of the silver plated frame, WM. EDGAR & R. M. SMITH, MINERAL POINT, WIS., presumably the makers. The large cylinder is a cluster of three small cylinders, each of which contains three chambers. It is manually turned until a slide on top of the frame will, when pushed forward, lock the gun so that the three chambers are in line with the three barrels which are rifled, about .34 caliber, and welded together. The barrels spread laterally apart at the muzzle so as to scatter the projectiles. The large cylinder has three nipples, one for each group of three chambers: All three chambers in each group receive fire from the exploded cap at the same time.

Many of the early multiple barrel guns designed to fire one shot at a time would fire the first two shots together if the operator moved a lever before pulling the trigger. The choice of whether there would be a single or double discharge was at the control of the operator, except in some seven-barrel flint pepperboxes where if all barrels were loaded, the one double discharge was unavoidable if the gun was fired until empty. The two-barrel pistol in figure 265 will fire first the left barrel and then the right, or both barrels simultaneously, depending on the positioning of the sliding lever on the side of the frame. The illustration shows the lever back and both flash pans open. The lever connects with a secondary pan cover which will slide over the right pan when the lever is moved forward. The frizzen is unusually wide, so it will serve as the primary cover for both pans. The pistol is by Durs Egg. The hallmark on the silver dates it 1786-7.

A final illustration of pistols with two barrels fired simultaneously is figure 266. From the standpoint of oddity these pistols are chiefly remarkable because they are in combination one with a knife and one with a fork. The combination of firearms with edged weapons has been a matter of course for centuries. The combination of flintlock pistols with tableware is less sensible.

These short barrelled, small caliber pistols are all metal, with brass frames. Both the knife and the fork are folding, like bayonets on blunderbusses. Each pistol has only one lock and one flash pan, but there are two vents in the pan, one on each side, so both barrels go off at the same time.

Examples of pistols combined with knives and forks are very scarce. The extraordinary and beautifully designed tableware in illustration 267 is probably the only existing set of knife, fork, and spoon all combined with pistols. The frames of these pistols are in bronze gilt, and bear the maker's name, F. X . RICHTER IN REICHEBERG. This superb trio normally reside in their original cloth covered wooden traveling case whose fitted interior is lined with velvet. The pistols date about 1715 and have lock mechanisms all on the outside, not concealed.

Completely exposed lock mechanisms may in themselves be considered sufficiently odd to warrant inclusion as curiosa. A

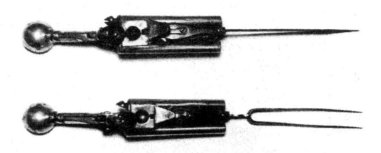

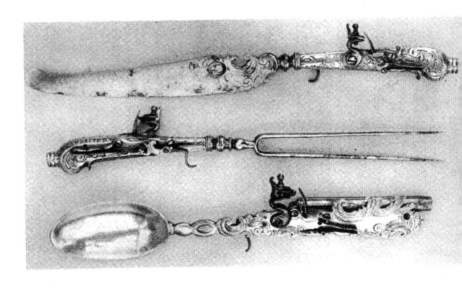

266. Knife and fork pistols/ Robert Abels collection.

267. Knife, fork and spoon pistols/ W. Keith Neal collection.

fine example of an all-metal pistol with the entire lock mechanism on the outside of the frame is shown in figures 268 and 269. The mechanism shown in the lower illustration, which is usually found attached to the inside of the lock plate, is of the simplest sort, consisting of mainspring, tumbler, sear and sear spring only.

I think it was Charles Winthrop Sawyer who styled flintlock tinderlighters, "the firearms that shed no blood." The two illustrated here are exceptions. Both are combined with pistols quite capable of shedding blood.

In illustration 270 there is shown an unmarked brass mounted table tinderlighter that can be quickly transformed into a pistol. As a tinderlighter the piece operates in normal fashion, the flint sending sparks into a small tinder-packed compartment, the tinder box. If the barrel which sticks out from this tinder box is charged with powder and ball, it may be fired if a round plate in the bottom of the box is turned until a hole in it lines up with a powder filled flash pan. With the tinder removed from the box the sparks from the flint will ignite the priming powder. Because of the length of the barrel, it is at once apparent this tinderlighter probably conceals a pistol. If the barrel had been made as short as possible the presence of the pistol might have gone unnoticed.

Not so with the combination piece in figure 271. This appears to be a two-shot, over-and-under, swivel breech, flint pistol. Actually, only one barrel is a pistol barrel. The other barrel is false, with a tinder box at the breech. The forward part of the false barrel is merely a receptacle, with a hinged cover at the muzzle, perhaps intended to hold tinder or possibly for use as a candle holder. The illustration shows the gun barrel in firing position. By pressing up and back on the trigger guard the barrel assembly may be turned over so the tinderlighter may operate. There is a triangular bayonet which may be released for use by pulling back a catch on the side of the frame. This pistol which conceals a tinderlighter is marked T. TOMSON a BRUXELLES.

Harpoons, rockets, life lines, bouquets of flowers, even human beings in a circus act have been projected from gun muzzles. In illustrations 272 and 273 are two pistols that were specially made to fire abnormal missiles. One has a barrel with a rectangular bore, about $\frac{7}{8}"$ x $\frac{1}{4}"$, and discharges a projectile shaped like a

268. and 269. Pistol with outside lock/ Murray M. Citrin collection.

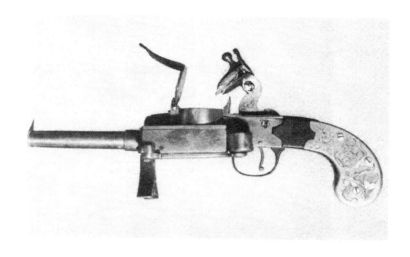

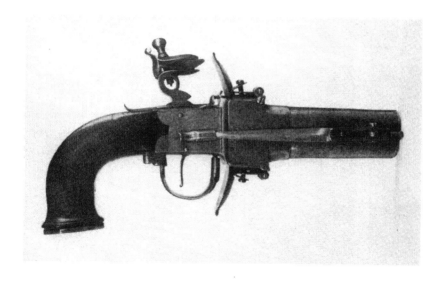

270. Tinderlighter pistol/ Dr. W. R. Funderburg collection.

271. Tinderlighter pistol—10" overall/ Frank R. Horner collection.

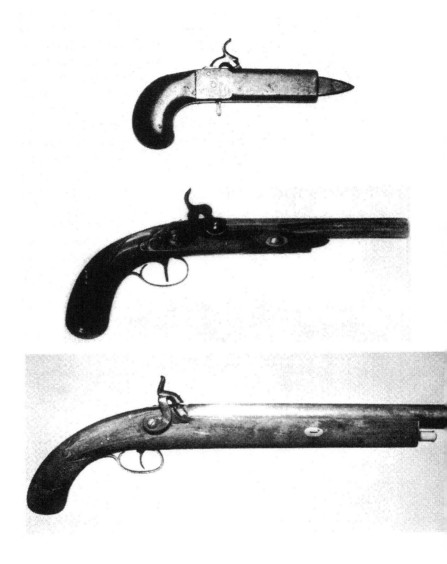

272. Knife shooting pistol/ Dr. W. R. Funderburg collection.

273. Arrow shooting pistol—12″ overall/ Frank Russell collection.

274. Magician's pistol/ Dr. W. R. Funderburg collection.

dagger point. The other shoots an arrow and has two twisting slots cut longitudinally through the barrel from the muzzle almost to the powder chamber. The slits are designed to hold two vanes of an arrow, so that when the pistol is fired the vanes will follow the twisting channels and cause the arrow to spin in flight.

A muzzle-loading magician's pistol that was constructed to be loaded with powder and ball and then to be fired without discharging the ball, is shown in figure 274. The large barrel that we see in the illustration is false. It has no vent to its powder chamber. The nipple vent actually leads the fire from the percussion cap around the false barrel to the powder chamber of a small true barrel disguised as a ramrod channel. The sleight of hand performer would have the false barrel loaded with powder and ball by a member of his audience in view of everyone. He would pretend to make sure the charge was well rammed down and then hand the pistol to an assistant, being careful to omit returning the ramrod. The hidden barrel had been previously loaded, with powder only of course. The assistant would fire across the stage aiming at the head of the performer, who would appear to catch the ball in his teeth.

Most guns with three or more barrels customarily have the barrels grouped around a central axis. Such guns include the pepperboxes and the modern German Drillings. Guns with three or more barrels in line, either vertically or horizontally, we usually class as oddities. The vertical arrangement of barrels was better liked than the horizontal, but no gun with three or more barrels in line ever came into high favor.

In figure 275 a noteworthy pair of three-barrel flintlock pistols by Griffin & Tow, London, is shown. The photograph gives a side view of one pistol and a top view of the other. It will be noticed there are three hammers and three frizzens but only two conventional triggers. The trigger of the lock that fires the middle barrel is a button in back of the sliding safety for the middle lock.

Another rare English three-barrel pistol, this one with the barrels in line vertically, is shown in figure 276. This is marked SMITH LONDON and has three nipples in a triangle. The unusual manually-turned striker is of the same design used on the Rigby knuckledusters illustrated in Chapter V.

A very unusual English percussion cap pistol that has ten

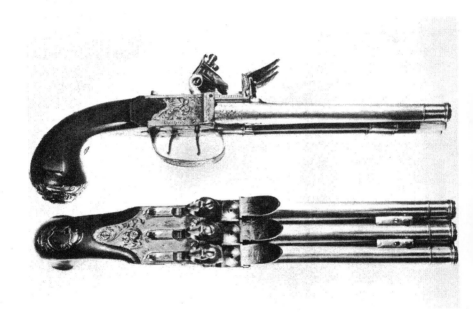

275. Pair Griffin & Tow pistols/ Henry M. Stewart collection.

barrels arranged in two tiers of five each is shown in figure 277. This was patented in England by R. & C. J. Jones, British patent #2351 of the year 1853. The gun illustrated is quite unmarked and may not have been made by the patentees but it looks exactly like the patent drawing and its construction fully agrees with the patent specification. There is but one trigger, but there are two hammers, two vertical rows of barrels and two rows of nipples. After the gun is loaded and capped, and the two hammers cocked, a trigger pull will drop the left hammer and fire the top barrel in the left tier. The next light trigger pull will slide the hammer back from the exploded cap and let a spring drive the hammer on the nipple next below. After the fifth pull has emptied the barrels on the left, the next pull will start the step-by-step descent of the hammer on the right.

An example of a Marston 3-barrel cartridge pistol is not hard to find. They were made in both .22 and .32 caliber models, some of which were fitted with short sliding daggers. These pistols are developments of a percussion cap 3-barrel pistol Mr. William W. Marston, of New York City, patented May 26, 1857, United States patent #17,386. (I have no photograph of one, and know of the existence of one only, of these percussion cap pistols.) Figure 278 illustrates an improved 1864 model in .32 caliber. The barrels are fired in ascending order by a firing pin which moves upward with the cocking of the hammer. There is a round turning piece, visible just ahead of the hammer, which is marked from 0 to 3 and has a pointer which indicates how many barrels have been fired. When the gun has been loaded the disc is turned until the pointer is at 0. Immediately in front of the disc is a three-pronged cartridge extractor, with which the earlier models were not equipped.

A modern pistol known as the Reform, even easier to find than a Marston, is shown in figure 279. This has four barrels, is double-action, and fires .25 ACP cartridges. The top barrel fires first. After that is fired another pull on the trigger raises the barrel block and fires the cartridge in the second barrel. Gas from this explosion escapes through a small hole into the top barrel and ejects the fired shell from that barrel. Each barrel is cleared when the cartridge in the barrel immediately below is discharged. The empty case in the lowest barrel is rammed out when the barrel block is removed for reloading. Because this gun

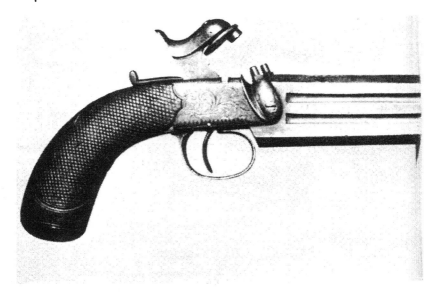

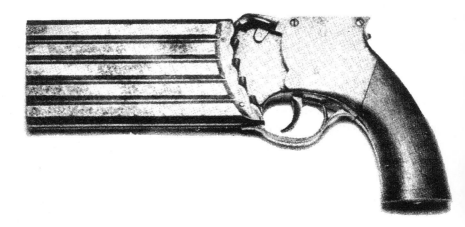

276. Three-barrel pistol—7" overall/ Sam E. Smith collection.

277. Ten-barrel pistol/ Photograph courtesy F. Theodore Dexter.

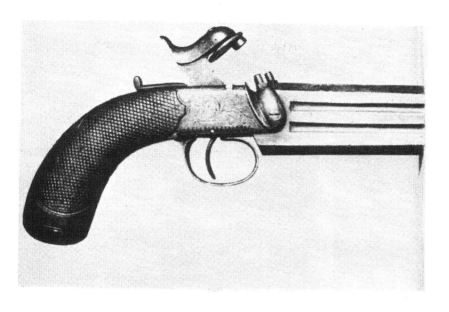

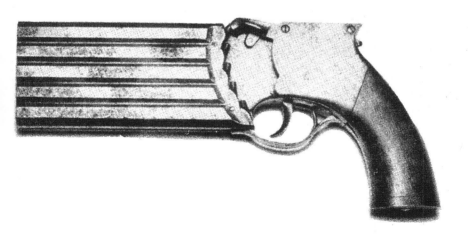

278. Marston pistol.
279. Reform pistol—5½″ overall.
280. Four-shot pistol/ Anthony A. Fidd collection.

is very thin and flat it has been popular on the Continent to carry in evening clothes.

Another even slimmer and more easily concealed 4-shot pistol is shown in figure 280. This unmarked French pistol is all steel and only $\frac{7}{16}''$ thick. The barrel block is hinged and tips up for loading. The four .22 caliber cartridges are hit in succession by a moving firing pin. Drawing out and pulling the folding trigger raises and drops the unobtrusive hammer.

The sliding barrel pistols that have gained most favor with collectors are the Jarre pistols commonly called simply "harmonicas." The pistols are of two types. The earlier type, United States patent #35,685, has a single barrel and a horizontally-sliding row of chambers; the later type, United States patent #137,927, has a horizontally-sliding row of barrels. The first patent was granted in 1862 to J. Jarre, of Paris, France; the second was granted in 1873 to A. E. and P. J. Jarre, both of Paris.

Figure 281 shows a single barrel Jarre pistol, photographed from below and at the side. The lock is double-action and trigger pressure moves the sliding breech-bar from left to right. The breech-bar holds ten pin-fire cartridges. A face plate, or yoke, holds the cartridges in position when the loaded breech-bar is secured in the frame. This plate is lifted for loading or unloading when the bar is removed from the frame.

Figures 282 and 283 show two Jarre pistols of the type described in the later patent. One of these has six barrels and is in firing position. The other has ten barrels and is in carrying position. Any of these multiple-barrel harmonica pistols can be put in the carrying position by pushing the barrel group, with the hammer held slightly raised, until the hammer is in line with the last barrel, and then turning and pivoting the group. An ejector rod is screwed in the butt of each of these short-barreled pistols.

These barrel blocks could be made with any number of bores. The inventor thought ten should be the limit.

The several guns just described which have sliding barrels or chambers have all been of modern cartridge type. A rare one with percussion cap ignition is in illustration 284. This is Belgian, marked H. COLLEYE BREVETE. The block has four chambers, each with a countersunk nipple, and is shown in position for the firing of the first shot. Pulling the ring trigger will raise the block, draw

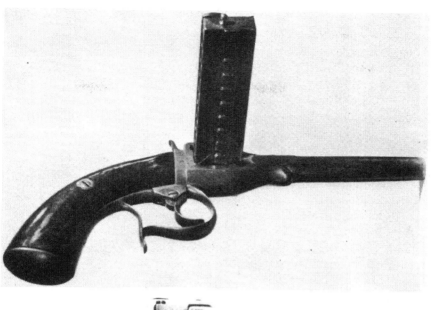

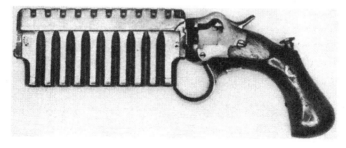

281. Ten-chamber harmonica—10″ overall/ Robert Abels collection.

282. Six-barrel harmonica.

283. Ten-barrel harmonica/ Henry M. Stewart collection.

back and drop the hammer.

A gun patented by Otto Schneelock of Brooklyn, on December 31, 1872, United States patent #134,442 is shown in figure 285. This uses a cartridge that is rarely seen and still more rarely identified. In fact, the gun itself is not noticed as being abnormal until one looks into the cylinder or down the barrel. As the invention has to do mainly with the boring of the cylinder, the gun is shown with the patent cylinder and one of its cartridges separate. At the right of the Schneelock cylinder is a conventional cylinder and one of its cartridges.

The Schneelock cylinder is bored to take cartridges having cases and bullets with isosceles triangle cross sections. Both cylinders illustrated have the same diameter. The Schneelock cylinder is slightly longer than the conventional cylinder. It holds seven bullets, each weighing 57 grains; the other cylinder also holds seven bullets, but these bullets weigh only 30 grains each. The gun appears to have a Smith & Wesson frame—third type of the first model .32—and the conventional cylinder illustrated is from such a gun. (The Smith & Wesson cylinder is of course fluted. The Schneelock cylinder is round.) The triangular bore of the Schneelock barrel is spirally cut. The ejecting rod is also triangular in cross section.

Perhaps the oddest point about the mortar pistol in illustration 286 is that collectors do not know the exact purpose of its unusually large barrel. Was it intended to serve as a signal pistol, a flare pistol, or to hurl either incendiary or explosive bombs? This Dutch pistol is stamped L. D. MEYER UTRECHT. The barrel is brass, 8½" long with a 1½" diameter bore, and has a round part about 6" in length which unscrews from the short octagonal part, to load whatever was used as a projectile.

Another pistol that is surely odd in appearance but which was developed for a purpose that is not now clear, is shown in figure 287. An old print shows the four outriders of a royal Spanish coach carrying guns similar in appearance. The enormous butt, over five inches in diameter, could serve as a club head. The belled muzzle might then help in grasping the gun. The barrel does not have a blunderbuss bore and the muzzle is of no practical value in shooting. The guns would make a parade more spectacular, and perhaps nothing more was required of them.

Most pepperboxes have four, five, or six barrels. Occasionally

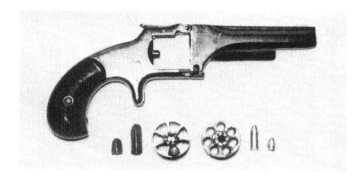

284. Colleye pistol—9″ overall/ Frank R. Horner collection.

285. Schneelock revolver/ Leo J. Werner collection.

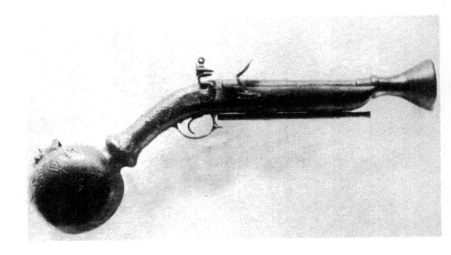

286. Mortar pistol—15½″ overall/ Sam E. Smith collection.

287. Outrider's gun/ Major Hugh Smiley collection.

we find one with eight barrels, but rarely with more than eight. One with twenty-four barrels is a curiosity. Of the few in existence, a fine example is shown in figure 288. This is a European ring trigger percussion cap Mariette with the barrels in two concentric rows, fifteen in the outer row and nine in the inner.

An American revolver with twenty-four chambers is shown in illustration 289. This piece was formerly in the Philo Remington collection and was designed by Fordyce Beals. I do not know of the existence of another example of this gun, or in fact of any other 24-shot American revolver. Revolvers having two barrels and with from fourteen to twenty chambers were described in an earlier chapter. This gun has twelve chambers in each of two rows, but it has only one barrel. The barrel, shown in position to guide bullets from the outer row, is pivoted near the muzzle and has a rotating lock at the breech end. The barrel may be depressed against spring pressure and locked in position to direct bullets from the inner row of chambers. The nipples are staggered and there is a rotating lock back of the hammer that may be set to limit the motion of the hand so the hammer will strike nipples in the inner row. The rammer has a double head that reaches both rows of chambers.

In illustration 290 is shown an all-metal folding revolver and in illustration 291 an all-metal folding pistol. Both guns are small and designed to be carried inconspicuously. The 5-shot revolver is Belgian and marked NOVO. It is double-action, hammerless and fires small low power cartridges. The thin curved metal grip may be put in the folded position shown when a stud is pressed. The folding pistol, figure 291, fires a single small caliber pin-fire cartridge and has several unusual features. It may be loaded by drawing back a pivoted breech section of the barrel when the gun is folded. After pulling up on the barrel muzzle until the barrel locks at a right angle to the frame, the gun may be cocked by pulling up the rear end of a heavy spring. This spring, which is screwed tight to the muzzle end of the barrel, acts as the striker to drive in the detonating pin of the cartridge. When the spring hammer is cocked, the gun may be fired by pressing a folding trigger which is attached to the barrel. The gun may be unlocked for folding when a button on the side of the frame is pressed. An ejecting rod is carried under the frame.

Perhaps as a result of the fact that some early American per-

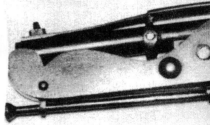

288. 24-shot pepperbox/ Paul Mitchell collection.
289. 24-shot revolver/ Henry M. Stewart collection.
290. Novo revolver/ Eddie Reider collection.
291. Folding pistol/ Dr. W. R. Funderburg collection.

cussion underhammer pistols had odd shaped grips and were carried in boot tops, some collectors class all underhammer pistols as oddities. The bootleg pistols do not have the beauty of fine Kentucky rifles, but they are equally worthy of collection as Americana and harder to find in good condition.

Three bootleg pistols are shown in illustration 292, two with hammers cocked. The top one is .41 caliber; the middle one .36; the bottom, .30. The one at the bottom is the most nearly conventional, in shape of grip and also in having the small star and diamond insets of silver.

In figure 293 is shown one of a pair of pistols, unmarked but believed to be American and probably made in Philadelphia. These finely made guns are short, but of heavy caliber, about .50.

A very unusual unmarked but apparently American underhammer pistol is in illustration 294. This has two swivel-breech, over-and-under barrels. There is a ring release to permit turning the solid breech block. The split trigger guard is also the mainspring.

A most peculiar underhammer percussion cap pistol is shown in figure 295. The illustration shows the barrel with the nipple on top and the front sight underneath. This position, necessary in order that a cap may be placed on the nipple, was reached by turning the barrel through 180° from its fired position. When the barrel is turned back the ring trigger will come forward, the hammer will be eased down and the pistol will be ready for double-action discharge by a pull on the ring trigger. After firing, the trigger will remain back until the barrel is again turned for recapping; it can not again assume the position for firing, which is double-action, until the barrel is turned both half around and then back. There is nothing missing in the picture. You can look right through the open space back of the barrel in the actual gun.

That pistol with the long underhammer extending forward from the grip has a complicated action. The two pistols shown in figure 296 solve the problem of making the nipple accessible for capping in a much simpler way. On each of these the long underhammer is attached to the barrel and is capable of being pushed to one side sufficiently to permit capping. One of these pistols, the top one, seems to be American; the other, completely unmarked, appears to be French. The top one bears the word "patent" as well as a name and a date, neither of which is clear.

292. Group bootleg pistols.

293. Underhammer pistol—7" overall/ Major Hugh Smiley collection.

294. Over-and-under pistol/ Major Hugh Smiley collection.

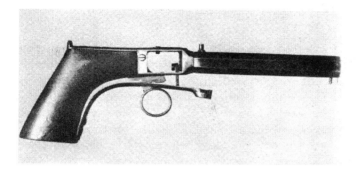

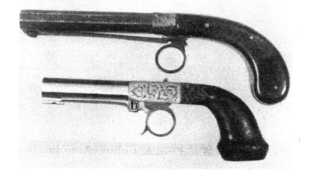

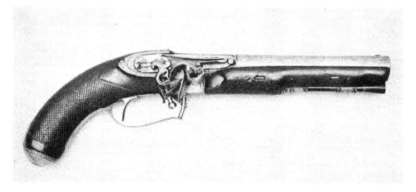

295. Underhammer pistol—10" overall/ Frank R. Horner collection.

296. Two underhammer pistols/ J. S. White collection.

297. Reversed flint pistol/ Metropolitan Museum of Art collection.

If the patent exists I overlooked it. Possibly an application was made and denied.

Each gun has only two moving parts. The lower gun operates the same as the upper, but is more expertly finished. When the spring hammer is pressed to the side the ring trigger falls away. The nipple is then capped, and the hammer and trigger moved back to the position in the illustration. Now when the trigger is pulled the spring hammer will be bent down until its end clears the lug on the trigger. The released hammer nose will then drive up and detonate the cap.

The pistol with the reversed flintlock, figure 297, is decidedly an oddity. The gun, by Tatham & Egg, London, is finely made and of heavy caliber, about .65. It was probably made on special order, but it is unlikely it was made just to prove it would work, for other guns exist with upside-down flintlocks.

Such guns as the Winchester, Marlin, Henry, Volcanic, have accustomed us to a magazine under, not over, the barrel A peculiarity of the repeating pistol illustrated in figure 298 is the location of the magazine above the barrel. The gun is usually called the gravity feed pistol. It fires a cartridge which is nothing more than a lead bullet hollowed at the base to hold a thin primer and a light charge of powder, quite like a Volcanic cartridge. The process of getting a cartridge from the magazine to the chamber requires first that the hammer be brought to half cock and left there until the cartridge is fully inserted in the chamber. Drawing the hammer to half cock raises the chamber block, or carrier, until the chamber is in line with the magazine. Pointing the muzzle up lets a cartridge slide down to the chamber. A very small rammer, operated with the thumb and forefinger, is provided to insure that the cartridge is pressed fully back. The illustration shows the gun at half cock with the little pivoted rammer having finished pushing the cartridge into the chamber. When the pistol is brought to full cock the carrier goes down, violently and with considerable noise, and aligns the loaded chamber with the barrel. The gun is Belgian, finely finished and ornamented. I can find no maker's name on the example illustrated.

In any repeating firearm that fires cartridges from a cylinder we confidently expect to find the barrel lined up with a chamber at the instant of firing. When the gun in figure 299 is fired the

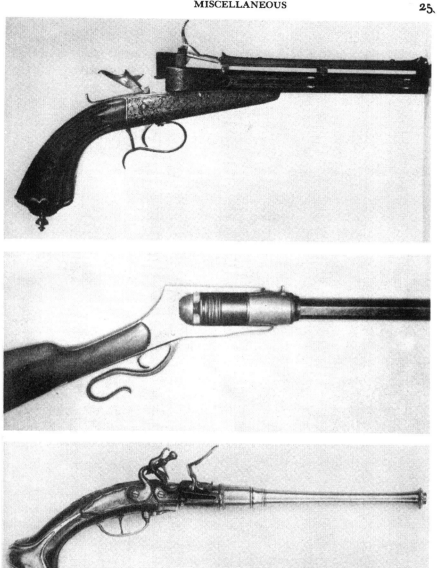

298. Gravity feed pistol—15" overall.

299. Morris & Brown/ Thomas J. McHugh collection.

300. Gorgo pistol/ Joseph Kindig, Jr. collection.

bullet must follow a curved path to get in the barrel. The gun illustrated was patented by William H. Morris and Charles L. Brown, of New York City, United States patent #26,919, dated January 24, 1860. The cylinder has six chambers for rim-fire cartridges which are fired by a revolving striker. The cylinder itself does not rotate. It may be moved out of the side of the frame for loading, and when returned to the frame it may be pressed forward and locked to make a gas-tight joint with the barrel breech. The extended and conical rear end of the barrel has six short passages converging from the six chamber mouths to the single bore of the barrel proper.

In figure 300 is a much earlier flintlock cylinder pistol, one of a pair, in which the bullets are well off center when discharged. In this gun the bullets are guided by a funnel and deflected into the barrel bore. The pistols, of masterly workmanship, are marked GORGO AT LONDON. Jackson, who illustrated this same pair, plate XXVII, in his *European Hand Firearms*, states, "The maker . . . to judge from the decorative design, was doubtless of Italian descent and probably domiciled in London during the second half of the XVIIth century". The cylinder is not stationary. It is revolved manually, when the trigger guard is pressed up, and has three chambers of about .40 caliber. The lock is equipped with a priming powder magazine operated by a lever attached to the frizzen.

Another exceptional piece, this by the English maker, Wilkinson, whose British patent for its features was 6139 of the year 1831, is shown in figures 301 and 302. This gun has several unusual features but its distinctive oddity is its special cartridge, designed to take full advantage of its elliptical blunderbuss barrel. The paper cartridge contains twelve quarter circle lead projectiles as well as a charge of powder and a thinly covered detonating cap. The twelve projectiles are formed by the mold illustrated. The pistol has a rising breech pivoted at the rear, like a Hall Army rifle. This is operated by a lever, at the top of the lock plate, which not only tilts the chamber but moves it backward and forward to give an obturating effect, like the movement of the cylinder on a Savage revolver. Before introducing the cartridge in the chamber the thin paper over the copper detonating cap is broken as the cap is pressed down on the nipple. If the special mold is not available the twelve projectiles

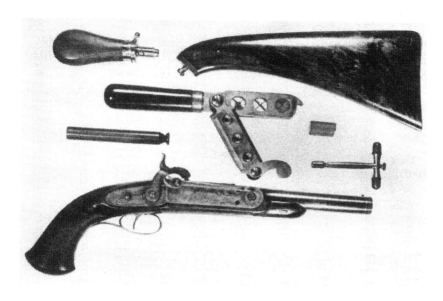

301. and 302. Wilkinson pistol—16″ overall/ Henry M. Stewart collection.

may be formed from a long cylinder of lead by two longitudinal and two transverse cuts. The inventor explains that these projectiles "will be so scattered laterally by the flattened bell shaped end of the barrel as to constitute a most formidable weapon of defence."

A blunderbuss was always esteemed as a weapon of defense, particularly by any highwayman who possessed one.

Francisco Xavier made the work of art shown in figure 303, just before 1800, in Spain. The steel is very finely and beautifully engraved, and the wood is artistically inlaid with silver. The three blades on this one-shot and one-barrel pistol certainly make it an oddity. There is a sliding penknife blade on top, a larger single-edge blade on the left, and a three-edged bayonet on the right. The one on top may be drawn back; the two on the sides may be folded back and secured.

In illustration 304 is an unmarked double-action 6-shot revolver, probably European, designed for use by a man who because of loss of fingers can not operate a conventional trigger.

There are four triggers on the gun in figure 305, which is the last photograph in this book of an actual gun. Any flintlock gun with more than two barrels, particularly if it has more than two triggers, is unusual. This fowling piece, with four barrels, four locks, and four triggers, is a finely designed gun by Le Compte a Chateaudun. The four 30" barrels are 24 gauge and are grouped around a center channel which holds the ramrod. The ramrod fits flush at the muzzle. There is a small stud on the side of the barrels to give it a push so it may be pulled out.

All illustrations that follow in this chapter are of patent drawings. The patent drawings illustrate strange creations which undoubtedly never were produced in quantity and of which I have located no example to photograph.

All quotations that appear under the patent drawing illustrations are taken from the related patent specifications.

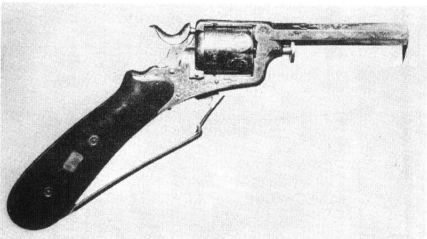

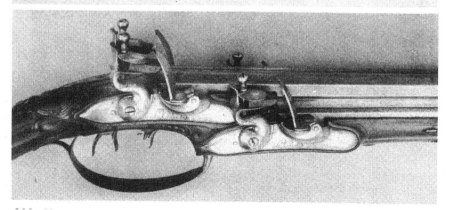

303. Xavier pistol/ Photograph reprinted by permission from *The Corpus and History of Hand Firearms* by Thomas T. Hoopes and William G. Renwick.

304. Fingerless pistol/ Dr. W. R. Funderburg collection.

305. Four-barrel gun/ W. Keith Neal collection.

Fig. 1.

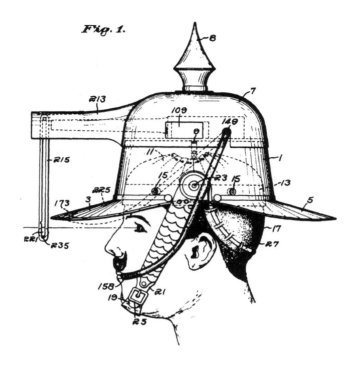

Inventor:
Albert B. Pratt,
by ~~~~~~~~~~~~~~~~~~
Attys.

ALBERT B. PRATT, OF LYNDON, VERMONT
U.S. Patent 1,183,492—WEAPON—May 16, 1916

306. Mr. Pratt considered that his combination of helmet and blowback automatic had many advantages. "The gun is automatically aimed . . . to the turning of the head of the marksman in the direction of the target . . . leaving his hands and feet free further to defend himself . . ." The crown may be detached, "inverted and used as a cooking utensil." The barrel cover becomes a handle, and the spike gives support in the ground. Blowing through a tube expands a pneumatic bulb which acts as a trigger. —I get headaches and I prefer to have someone else test the gun, though Mr. Pratt is confident the two movements of the blowback breech-bolt "naturalize (*sic*) one another . . . no discomfort . . . from the recoil."

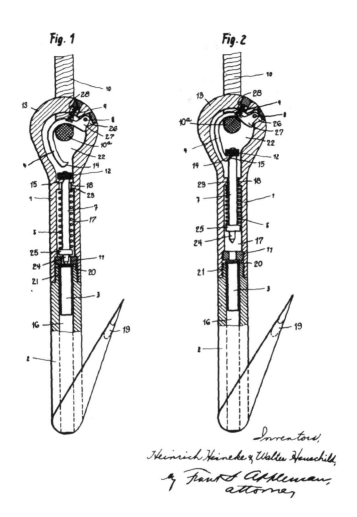

Fig. 1   Fig. 2

Inventors,
Heinrich Heineke & Walter Hauschild,
by Frank S. Appleman,
attorney,

H. HEINEKE ET AL, GERMANY
U.S. Patent 2,253,125—FISHING HOOK—Aug. 19, 1941

307. A firing mechanism entirely encased in the hook so the fish will "not be frightened away without biting" and so aimed that when ". . . a fish gives a sudden jerk on the hook . . . .the firing pin will be released to strike the cartridge and the latter will be discharged, thus killing or stunning the fish." ——Might have caught the big one that got away.

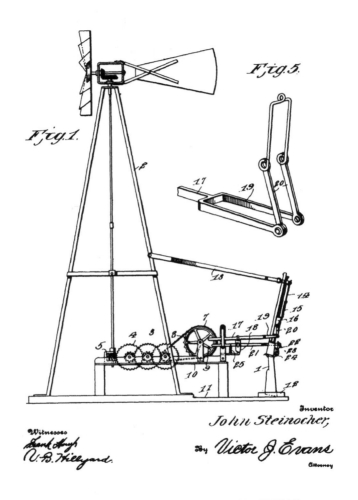

JOHN STEINOCHER, OF WEST, TEXAS
U.S. Patent 1,056,602—AUTOMATIC GUN FIRING MECHANISM
Mar. 18, 1913.

308. A mechanical scarecrow "for scaring off birds, animals and such like as tend to prey upon or devastate crops, stock or like property" with ". . . novel mechanism for discharging the fire arm at predetermined intervals . . ."—A high wind would keep an attendant busy refilling the magazine.

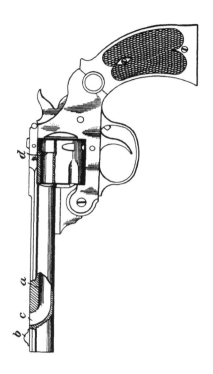

J. E. BANNER, OF MOUNT AIRY, NORTH CAROLINA
U.S. Patent 1,007,174—STAGE FIREARM—Oct. 31, 1911

309. A pistol which ". . . may be used for stage purposes without the possibility of harming any of the actors or stage hands and at the same time which will permit the weapon to be aimed directly and deliberately at the actor . . . thus enabling a more realistic exhibition . . ." and ". . . thus avoiding the farcical exhibitions now commonly seen on the stage . . ."——Harmless deception that seems a good idea.

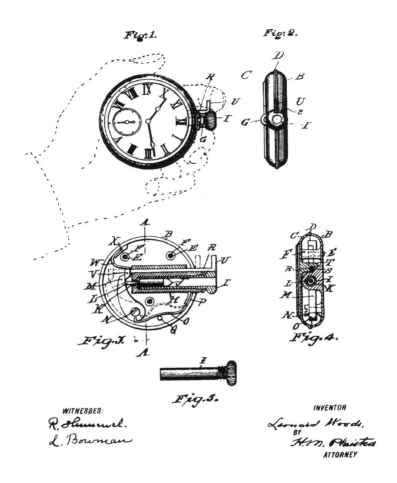

Fig. 1.

Fig. 2.

Fig. 3.

Fig. 4.

Fig. 5.

WITNESSES:
R. Hummel.
L. Bowman

INVENTOR
Leonard Woods,
BY
H. M. Plaisted
ATTORNEY

LEONARD WOODS, OF ST. LOUIS, MISSOURI
U.S. Patent 1,073,312—PISTOL—September 16, 1913

310. "The object of my invention is to provide a pistol that can be carried in the vest pocket like a watch, is as readily accessible, and appears like a watch, whereby it may be presented and fired at a highwayman while apparently merely obeying his command to 'hand over your watch and be quick about it'!"

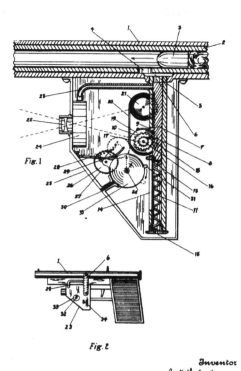

Fig. 1

Fig. 2

Inventor
Adalbert Szalardi

ADALBERT SZALARDI, OF NEW YORK, N. Y.
U.S. Patent 1,550,849—CAMERA GUN—Aug. 25, 1925

311. "It very often happens that policemen, military persons, but even private people are obliged to use guns for self defense. After such an occurrence the courts usually have to determine the legality or necessity of the use of guns and have to depend on witnesses, if any, who are very often absolutely unreliable . . . Fleeing automobiles with the criminals therein and so on may also be photographed while being shot at." —— There is a clock in the camera. The film notes the time the subject is shot, literally or figuratively. The inventor recommends using magnesium with the gun powder, to provide light for taking pictures at night.

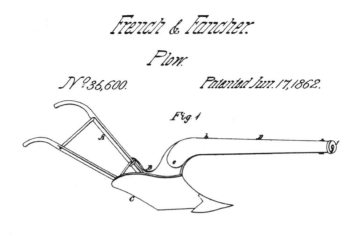

French & Fancher.

Plow.

Nº 35,600.   *Patented Jun. 17, 1862.*

Fig 1

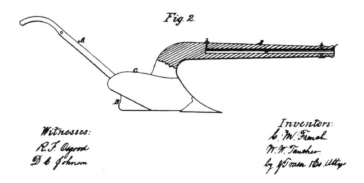

Fig. 2.

Witnesses:
R. J. Osgood
D. C. Johnson

Inventors:
C. M. French
W. H. Fancher
by J. Smith his Atty

C. M. FRENCH AND W. H. FANCHER, OF WATERLOO, NEW YORK
U.S. Patent 35,600—PLOW—June 17, 1862

312. "Ordnance Plow . . . a means of defense in repelling surprises and skirmishing attacks on those engaged in a peaceful avocation it is unrivaled . . . The share serves to anchor it firmly in the ground." —— Just unharness the team and shoot.

A.D. 1897. Dec. 24. N°. 30,525.
ANGRESS' Complete Specification.

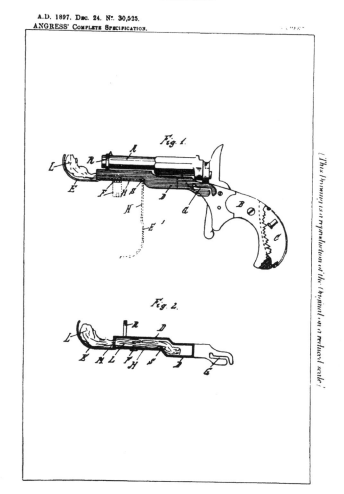

Fig. 1.

Fig. 2.

WILLIAM ANGRESS, UPPER SILESIA
An Improved Igniting Device for Cycle Lamps.
British patent—A. D. 1897. Dec. 24, No. 30,525

313. "The benzine match container D in which is situated a priming or tinder match L saturated with readily ignitable liquid, has a bottom H which can be made to fold down on a hinge S and which is itself fixed by means of a fastening F to the benzine match container . . . In order to light the lamp, a percussion cap is placed in the firearm . . . When it is desired to employ the firearm A directly as such, it is merely necessary to turn down the lower part of the tinder container with its nose, whereupon the muzzle of the barrel of the firearm is free." —— It would still make an interesting cigarette lighter.

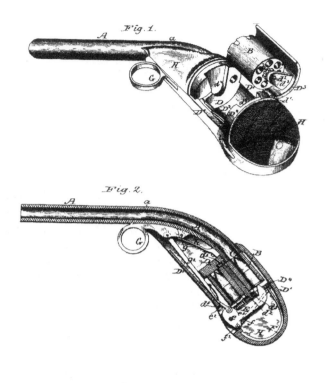

Fig. 1.

Fig. 2.

Witnesses.
E.E. Wurdeman.
W.B. Masson.

Inventor.
William H. Sprague,
By his attorney.
E.E. Masson.

WILLIAM H. SPRAGUE, OF JAMESTOWN, NEW YORK
U.S. Patent 380,361—REVOLVER—Apr. 3, 1888

314. " . . . rendering the complete fire-arm more compact, lessening the weight of pocket arms, and making them more convenient in use and transportation" were the objects of Mr. Sprague's invention of this curved barrel revolver. —— A precursor of the curved barrel guns that shot around corners in World War II.

Chapter 12

FANCY FREE

THE PHOTOGRAPHS in the previous chapters showed actual guns, conceived in all seriousness. The drawings reproduced in this chapter are of unreal guns and fictitious advertisements, conceived in fun. Colt's Manufacturing Company never made, and never will make, any such pistols or revolvers.

Stephen Ickes, with considerable humor and imagination, drew these fantastic guns in fine detail for his own amusement and the mystification of Robert Abels. He sent the unsigned originals to Mr. Abels one at a time at odd intervals, and did not identify himself as the artist for a year or more.

The "New Apex" may puzzle some readers. The upper cylinder contains six chambers, one for each of the various cartridges. The lower cylinder contains six barrel bores, of six different calibers, one to match each chamber. The mechanism required to make the cylinders rotate in unison is very simple. No thought whatever has been given to it.

No further information will be released on any of these Fancy Free revolvers until after the return of the first space ship to visit Mars.

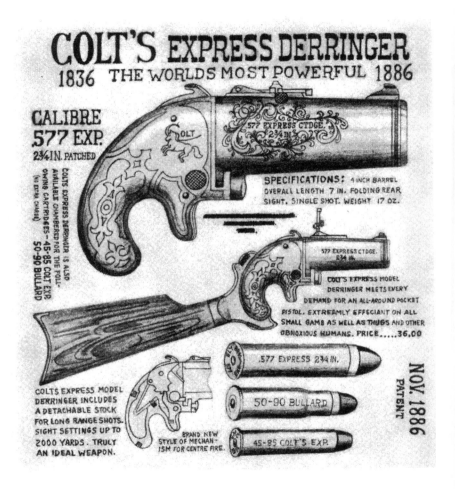

315. IMAGINARY ONLY

316. IMAGINARY ONLY

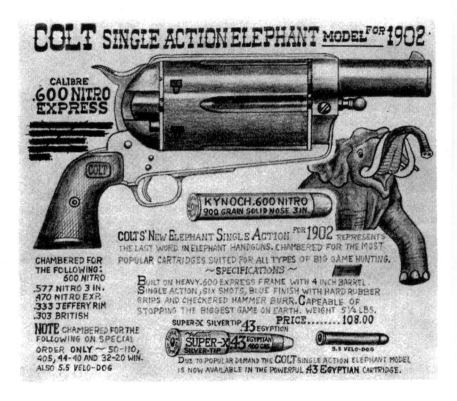

317. IMAGINARY ONLY

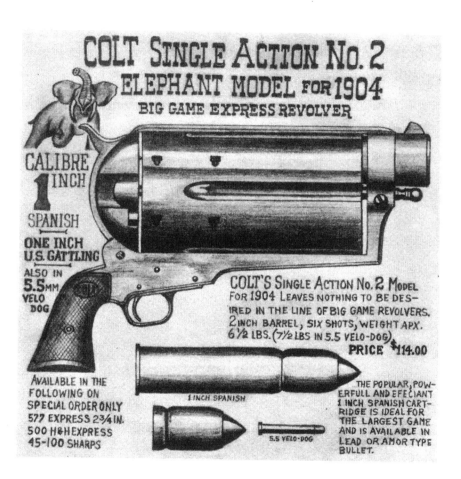

318. IMAGINARY ONLY

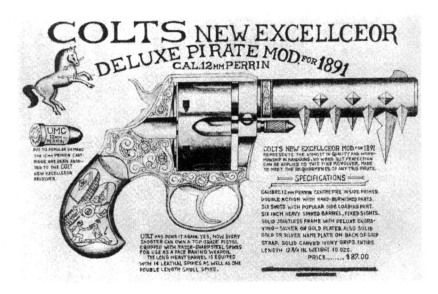

319. IMAGINARY ONLY

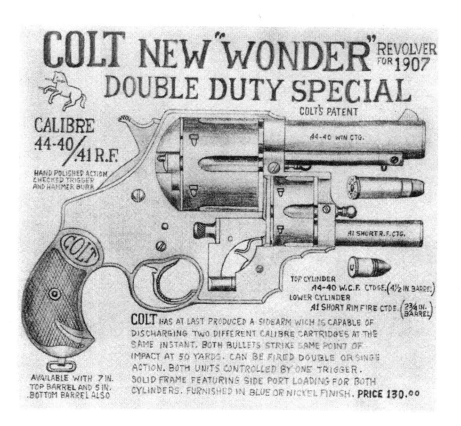

320. IMAGINARY ONLY

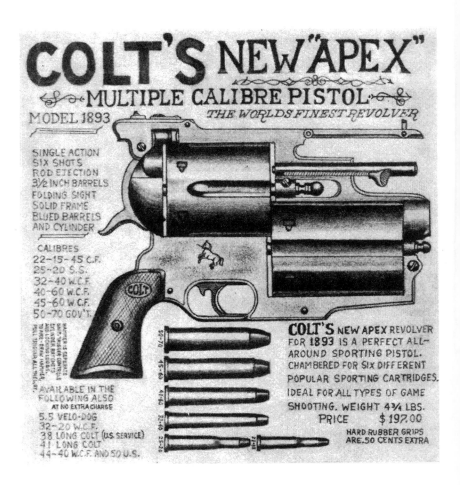

321. IMAGINARY ONLY

BIBLIOGRAPHY

ABELS, ROBERT. *Early American Firearms*. Cleveland, 1950.

A GENTLEMAN OF PHILADELPHIA COUNTY. *The American Shooter's Manual*. Philadelphia, 1827.

The American Rifleman. (Periodical) Various Issues.

Antiques. (Periodical) Various Issues.

Army and Navy Journal. (Periodical) Various Issues.

BOCK, GERHARD. *Moderne Faustfeuerwaffen und Ihr Gebrauch*. Neudamm, 1911.

CHINN, LT. COL. GEORGE M. *The Machine Gun*. Washington, 1951.

DEANE, J. *Deane's Manual of the History and Science of Fire-Arms*. London, 1858.

DEMMIN, AUGUST. *Die Kriegswaffen*. Leipzig, 1893.

DEXTER, F. THEODORE. *Thirty-Five Years Scrapbook of Antique Arms*. Topeka, 1947.

DEXTER, F. THEODORE. *Rare Ancient Arms*. Los Angeles, 1954.

FFOULKES, CHARLES J. *Inventory and Survey of the Armouries of the Tower of London*. London, 1916.

GEORGE, JOHN NIGEL. *English Pistols and Revolvers*. Onslow County, North Carolina, 1938.

GEORGE, JOHN NIGEL. *English Guns and Rifles*. Plantersville, South Carolina, 1947.

GLUCKMAN, MAJOR ARCADI. *United States Martial Pistols and Revolvers*. Buffalo, 1939.

GLUCKMAN, COLONEL ARCADI. *United States Muskets, Rifles and Carbines*. Buffalo, 1948.

GREENER, WILLIAM WELLINGTON. *The Gun and Its Development*. London, 1881.

The Gun Collector. (Periodical) Various Issues.

The Gun Report. (Periodical) Various Issues. Published 1939 to 1942.

HAVEN, CHARLES T. and BELDEN, FRANK A. *A History of the Colt Revolver.* New York, 1940.

HEWITT, JOHN. *Ancient Armour and Weapons in Europe.* London, 1860 edition.

JACKSON, HERBERT J. *European Hand Firearms of the Sixteenth, Seventeenth, & Eighteenth Centuries.* London, 1923.

LOGAN, HERSCHEL C. *Hand Cannon to Automatic.* Huntington, W. Va., 1944.

Magazine of Antique Firearms. (Periodical) Published 1911 to 1912.

METSCHL, JOHN. *The Rudolph J. Nunnemacher Collection of Projectile Arms.* Milwaukee, 1928.

OMMUNDSEN, H. and ROBINSON, ERNEST H. *Rifles and Ammunition.* London, 1915.

PARSONS, JOHN E. *Henry Deringer's Pocket Pistol.* New York, 1952.

POLLARD, MAJOR HUGH BERTIE CAMPBELL. *A History of Firearms.* London, 1926.

ROBERTS, NED H. *The Muzzle-Loading Cap Lock Rifle.* Manchester, N. H., 1940.

SATTERLEE, L. D. *A Catalog of Firearms for the Collector.* Detroit, 1927.

SAWYER, CHARLES WINTHROP. *Firearms in American History; 1600 to 1800.* Boston, 1910.

SAWYER, CHARLES WINTHROP. *Firearms in American History. Vol. II. The Revolver, 1800 to 1911.* Boston, 1911.

SAWYER, CHARLES WINTHROP. *United States Single Shot Martial Pistols.* Boston, 1913.

SAWYER, CHARLES WINTHROP. *Our Rifles.* Boston, 1920.

Scientific American. (Periodical) Various Issues.

SCOTT, SIR WALTER. *Rob Roy.*

SERVEN, JAMES E. *Paterson Pistols.* Dallas, 1946.

SERVEN, JAMES E. *Colt Dragoon Pistols.* Dallas, 1947.

SERVEN, JAMES E. *Colt Percussion Pistols.* Dallas, 1947.

SERVEN, JAMES E. *Colt Cartridge Pistols.* Santa Ana, 1952.

SHARPE, PHILIP B. *The Rifle in America.* New York, 1938.

SMITH, WALTER H. B. *Pistols & Revolvers.* Harrisburg, 1946.

STEUART, RICHARD D. and FULLER, CLAUD E. *Firearms of the Confederacy.* Huntington, W. Va., 1944.

STONE, GEORGE CAMERON. *A Glossary of the Construction, Decoration and Use of Arms and Armor.* Portland, Maine, 1934.

THIERBACH, M. *Die Geschichtliche Entwickelung der Handfeuerwaffen.* Dresden, 1888.

VAN RENSSELAER, STEPHEN. *American Firearms.* Watkins Glen, N. Y., 1947.

INDEX

All Right Fire Arms Co., 84
Allen, C. B., 32, 196
American Portable Burglar Alarm, 102
Ames Sword Co., 80
Andrews, R. W., 36
Angress, William, 267
Apache Knuckleduster, 90
Arrow projectile, 239
Axe, 21

Banner, J. E., 263
Bar pistol, 70
Barbar, 226
Battleaxe, 21
Bazar, 130
Beals, Fordyce, 249
Beauregard, General, 58
Bechtler, C., 210
Beerstecher, Frederick, 180
Bell and gun, 108
Belt buckle pistol, 151
Belt pistol, 151
Belton, Joseph, 176
Bicycle handlebar pepperbox, 154
Billinghurst, William, 54
Blow gun, 144
Boardman, Edward, 84
Bootleg pistol, 251
Bowie knife, 27, 32
Bruni, Pietro, 18
Buckler, 11
Buco, 162
Burglar alarm, 100

Calendar sword, 16
Camera gun, 265
Campbell, James C., 40
Canteen stock, 221
Cardiff, Charles, 167
Chaffee, Noah, 100
Chambers, Joseph, 167, 171
Chesebrough, B. F., 100
Chicago Fire Arms Co., 78
"Chicken thief", 112
Child, Joseph, 53
Chopper, 16, 23
Christ, Albert, 62
Clockwork alarm, 97
Cochran, John W., 196
Coffee mill, 221
Colleye, H., 244

Colt, 25, 90, 221, 269
Colvin, Robert J., 34
Conklin & Hauser, 104
Coon, David, 100
Coon, Simeon, 100
Cottrell, S. P., 162
Crossbow, 21
Cuirass, 12
Curved barrel revolver, 268
Cutlass (Elgin), 27
Cycle lamp gun, 267

Dagger pistol, 16, 18, 226
Dagger projectile, 239
Daigle, Marcelin, 144
Davis, Walter, 40
Day, John, 136, 154
Defender, 124
Delhaxhe, 90
Dolne, L., 90
Door alarm, 97, 106
Door stop alarm, 106
Dosick, Samuel, 52
Double Deringer, 186
Double Ender, 210, 215
Double Header, 217
Double Ignition, 226
Double-jaw hammer, 225
Douglas, Sir Howard, 225
Dreyse, 214
Duckfoot, 228

Egg, Durs, 233
Elgin, George, 27
Elliot, 184
Ellis, Reuben, 174
Enouy, Joseph, 208
Espingole, 170

Ferris, Hudson, 104
Ferris wheel, 208
Finnegan, Peter H., 78
Fisher Firesure, 52
Fishing hook, 261
Fist gun, 223
Flashlight revolver, 162
Fore and aft, 210
Forsyth, Alexander, 23, 54
Foster, George, 201
Frankenau, 157
French & Fancher, 266

Printed in Great
Britain
by Amazon